P9-BXY-525

THE
UNPOPULAR
MISSIONARY

Ralph E. Dodge

THE
UNPOPULAR
MISSIONARY

FLEMING H. REVELL COMPANY

Acknowledgment is made to Henry Weman, Cathedral Organist, Upsala Theol. Dr, for permission to reprint portions of his book, *African Music and the Church in Africa* (Upsala, Sweden, Svenska Institutet for Missionsforskning, 1960).

The Scripture quotations in this publication so identified are from the *Revised Standard Version of the Bible*, copyrighted 1946 and 1952 by the Division of Christian Education, National Council of Churches, and used by permission.

Dedicated to
MY MOTHER
Lizzie Longshore Dodge

Foreword

If you think there is nothing wrong with Christian missions, you should not read this book. But if you happen to be one of those who still think the missionary effort can win if we have the good sense and the courage to correct what is wrong and make a new start with what is right, you'd better read it.

In the minds of millions of us is the gnawing question, "Have missions failed?" China is closed to us, the future in India is uncertain; and with the African rising to take the reins of control from the white man and rule his own land, the missionary in Africa faces what seems to be an impossible situation. After a century of consecrated effort, many are fearful that we may have come to the end of the great crusade.

Few men in Christendom are better qualified or in a better position to understand all this than is the author of this book. He has served long years as a missionary; in 1956 he was elected Bishop of Angola, Rhodesia and Southeast Africa—the first Methodist bishop to be elected *in Africa*. He speaks with authority. He knows at firsthand what is and has been wrong, and what he has to say about that has never been said in such language before; it is not conducive to complacency or a good night's sleep, but it happens to be true.

He is not despondently negative about it. He writes in grateful acknowledgment of the work, spirit and sacrifice of those who were missionaries before him and who lie buried in some corner of a forgotten foreign field that is forever Christ's because they came and served and died. And finally he tells what must be done if their sacrifice is not to be in vain, and the whole cause lost.

Throughout, it is the most disturbing and strengthening book on missions that we have read in many a year. All who read it will not agree with all of it—any more than all who read the Bible agree on all of that—but all will be conscious of a challenge in it, the acceptance of which will spell the difference between dismal failure in our futile allegiance to outmoded techniques and outdated philosophies, and ultimate triumph for Christ in the blazing of new trails in a very new and different world.

A great crucial hour has struck in the march of man; it is indeed five minutes to twelve, especially on the missionary clock. What we do at this hour may be as fateful as what the first Christian missionaries decided to do two thousand years ago. Now, *right now*, we determine whether it is to be "Missionary, go home!" or "Missionary, come back!"—later.

This book is a guide for our moment of decision, written by one not blind but quite awake, troubled and concerned, yet certain of the light that comes always after the night of storm.

THE PUBLISHERS

Preface

This book is written with the hope that it may be considered a plan of action for the future. Many Europeans in Africa will undoubtedly consider me unfair in my evaluation of situations and events and consequently label me pro-African. Many African nationalists will consider my reactions typically European. If the conclusions are denounced on all sides, I will have achieved a fair degree of objectivity.

The word "European," as used in southern Africa, means all white people—including Americans. The word "politics" has the more inclusive meaning of community or social involvement.

I wish to express my thanks to my two secretaries, William James Humbane and Robert Lee Stuart, for their devoted help. The former transcribed innumerable discs, first putting the author's rambling thoughts on paper; the latter organized and edited the material, bringing order out of chaos. Mrs. Mary Phil Higgs and Mrs. Mava Stine were especially helpful in criticizing the manuscript.

Heartfelt appreciation goes to my wife, Eunice Elvira Dodge, for her willingness to share with me the many pleasant, and few bitter, experiences in Africa. Without her encouragement, this manuscript would never have been written.

Finally, to those many Africans whose names are not recorded, but who have shared their concern about the church in Africa, goes my special gratitude.

Ralph E. Dodge

SALISBURY, SOUTHERN RHODESIA

Contents

PART III—*The Church and Its Future*

THE CHURCH MUST:

Part I

THE CHURCH AND ITS CRITICS

THE CHURCH UNDER FIRE

The Christian church is under fire in Africa. But there is nothing novel or surprising in this fact since the church has always progressed in the face of fear, antagonism, jealousy, bewilderment, indifference, and even contempt. The Christian church in Africa has been no exception to this historic role. It has faced opposition from entrenched animism and Islam, from jealous chiefs, from suspicious tribesmen, from self-seeking colonials, from ardent nationalists, from over-zealous reformers, and even from so-called Christian governments.

For decades missionaries have gone home to their supporting constituencies with wonderful stories regarding the effectiveness of the Christian witness in Africa. If a local church had difficulties and doubts, if the younger generation seemed calloused to the teachings of Christ, if the minister was discouraged or unpopular—congregations in America and Europe could reassure themselves with the thought that all was well on the mission field. In Africa, at least, the church was a fellowship of the faithful; the Bible brought unity, comfort and peace; Christ lived again in the lives of noble missionaries and saintly African Christians. The popularity of this half-truth has served to obscure the inadequacies of both the church at home and the church in Africa.

Because of this well-publicized success story, the present wave of antagonism has come as a surprise to many Christians around the world. But the surprise often gives way to dismay and discouragement when the older churches discover that severe criticism of the church in Africa today comes from *within*—it comes from second-generation Christians, and it comes with a force and bitterness that is convincing. All is *not* well on the mission field.

It is not unusual for new missionaries in Africa today to become disillusioned when they discover that the very people they come to serve regard them with suspicion, nor for churches in Europe and America to be disheartened when mission "products" are bitterly disposed toward them, nor for veteran missionaries to retire early because of the "ingratitude" of their African charges.

Young Africa believes that its church has grave faults which need to be corrected if the Word of God is to be effective. This criticism indicates that the church in Africa may become a healthy church, dissatisfied with the status quo, unhappy over past mistakes, impatient to improve and eager for a more effective witness.

What has the church of Christ done that it should merit such criticism from its own members? What challenge does this criticism present to the church today as it reaches forward to make its witness effective in the future?

1

Colonialism

"*MANY OF THE* churches of this country are agents of government in the oppression of the African people. . . ."

"There is always conflict between a missionary and an African Christian; the latter wants both Christianity and freedom from colonial powers. There are some missionaries who support colonial power."

"The Christian missionaries accommodated themselves to the psychology of the colonizers."

The chorus is swelling; the criticisms by African youth become increasingly severe. Harsh as they may be, the criticisms are made in the interest of the church. In dealing with these criticisms (made largely by those within the church), one must realize that these charges are considerably more moderate than those made by people outside of the Christian community. Unless they are listened to, unless they are taken seriously, unless changes are made, those now making criticisms from the "inside" will join the ranks of those "outside"—who seek not to reform the church, but to destroy it.

Within the leadership of the church itself, there are at least three different reactions to the current avalanche of criticism. One group hears only the violence of the criticism and concludes that the people of Africa have been led away from the church by various evil influences. They sigh for the bygone days when the African people were eager to hear the "white man's message," and they denounce present-day attitudes as unnatural. They claim that nationalism, or education, or communism has blighted the "innocence" of Africa. They feel, not that the church has failed, but that outside forces have corrupted the African people.

The second group is comprised of those who argue that, although the church may have made mistakes in the past, her basic position is sound. They hear the criticism as an historical phenomenon accompanying the rise of political and social consciousness. History indicates that there is often a falling-away from the true church during a time of strain, especially among second-generation Christians; thus, the number of Africans who criticize and leave the church today serves to indicate the stress and strain of the times. The duty of the church in such times, this group maintains, is to ignore or deny the validity of the criticisms made against it and to continue preaching the gospel as if nothing unusual were happening.

The third group is the only one that listens to criticism and welcomes it in the hope that it can be used to correct past mistakes, and to help guide the future direction of the church. They realize that the church of Christ is composed of human beings who are subject to error. They acknowledge the place of reformation and in humility carefully consider all criticism against the church, accepting what is valid and opposing and correcting what is false.

Only by taking this last position can the church in Africa find a way to become truly effective in meeting the needs of African Christians in the modern world. Criticism can be a very healthy sign. Missionaries who feel the sting of criticism may think it unjust that their mistakes receive more attention than do their achievements. But one should never forget that the church of Christ in Africa will not be built by foreign missionaries. It will be built by Christ. The church in Africa will come into its own on that day when African Christians are a body under Christ, rather than under a foreign Board of Missions, or even under the World Council of Churches.

An African student writes: "We are fighting a decisive war against all forms of colonialism and foreign domination and the missionary cannot safely take a theoretical approach to both our economic and political problems." The church must listen and the church must *act*.

A Rhodesian Christian studying in India has written that one of his non-Christian African friends there is convinced that "the church is an agent of foreign rule. It was in most cases the missionaries who were forerunners of the imperialists. The missionaries were sent ahead to negotiate with the chiefs and to persuade them to sign treaties and concessions."

Although the charge that early missionaries were conscious "softening-up" agents for colonial interests would be difficult to sustain, the close relationship which has existed between the church and colonial governments cannot be ignored. It must be admitted that missionaries generally share four things with colonial government agents: common nationality and culture, common race, administrative authority, and a position of privilege.

In most African countries a majority of missionaries are of the same nationality as the colonial administrators. Most missionaries in Portuguese Africa are Roman Catholics from Portugal. The largest single national group of missionaries in Commonwealth countries are of British descent. Even in that spiritual happy-hunting-ground for missionaries from all over the world—the former Belgian Congo—the largest single group of missionaries prior to independence were Belgian Roman Catholics. It is not surprising, therefore, that in each case there is a prevailing sympathy and closeness of relationship between colonial administrators and national missionaries. This means that in their cultural background, general outlook, and personal sympathy they tend to uphold the political position and colonizing policy of the countries from which they come. Missionaries are like everyone else—children of their own cultures. National loyalties become all the stronger when they come into contact with people of other traditions.

In Angola the Roman Catholic Archbishop's office is adjacent to the Governor General's and reportedly there is full consultation on all matters of national interest. In Angola and Mozambique, by an agreement between Lisbon and the Vatican, nearly all African education is turned over to the Roman Catholic Church, which gets much of its support from public funds. Portuguese Roman Catholics inculcate loyalty to Portugal in their teaching, say the officials; for the same reason, the government also requires Protestant missions to employ at least one Portuguese national in each school.

When the nationalist uprising occurred in Angola in early 1961, the Archbishop in Luanda made a statement published in *Apostolado* (official organ of the archdiocese), condemning the Angola nationalists and supporting the government. There are other Catholics, however, who have actively supported the nationalists.

Several years ago when I visited a Methodist primary school in Elisabethville, Katanga province of Congo, the headmaster (a Belgian Protestant) showed me around the school. I tried to establish contact with pupils in the upper class by asking them what they planned to do when they finished the education available to them in that particular school. Some indicated that they would be masons; others, carpenters; a few, clerks and teachers. One lad "brought down the house" when he suggested that he wanted to be an airplane pilot. Emboldened by that departure from the established norm, another boy raised his hand and said that he wanted to be a doctor. The European headmaster reprimanded him immediately for his ambitious desire: "He means that he plans on being a nursing orderly. In the Congo we do not have native doctors." And there the matter rested—until independence!

At that time, the Belgian government did not look kindly upon Africans entering professions requiring training outside the Congo. Therefore, churchmen of all nationalities generally accommodated themselves to the official viewpoint. Thus when independence came few Africans were prepared for the responsibilities.

Often non-national church leaders lean over backward adapting themselves to the psychology of the colonizing countries and like many U.S. northerners transplanted to southern states, they adopt a harsh and uncompromising attitude toward all Negroes —they fear the brand of "liberals." In a similar way European churchmen may be less flexible in relationships with Africans than are government officials.

Not long ago, a European missionary said that he could work cooperatively with the African people in the church so long as violence did not break out. Should there be violence, his loyalties were such that he would answer the call of his country to take up arms. This is an unusual case, but often the entire missionary force is judged by a few isolated and extreme cases.

Because most missionaries belong to the same race as the original colonizers and government agents in power, the African masses tend to repudiate them and their teaching. Only a comparatively few white people have been able to break out of their racial classification to become labeled "white Africans."

Although no official statement has been made (so far as I know), it is generally believed that non-Caucasian male missionaries are unwelcome in some parts of Africa. Perhaps governments think that American Negroes, for instance, might more easily identify themselves with the local population in a time of national disturbance or that their very presence might tend to give the local people ideas of equality.

Before Congo independence, it was understood that the Belgian authorities would not welcome male Negroes as missionaries although both there and in Angola Negro women missionaries were tolerated. The Federation of Rhodesia and Nyasaland has refused at least one Negro missionary applicant and granted only temporary residence to the Negro bishop of the African Methodist Episcopal Church.

White missionaries, in turn, have at times been reluctant to receive nonwhite colleagues, partly because of the discrimination which Negroes would have to suffer, and partly because of the embarrassment which they might cause their colleagues in a segregated society.

The Pan-African Nationalist movement is partially racial as well as partially nationalistic. As it reaches the apex of its strength in its drive for independence within any given country, there is apt to be discrimination; violence may even be used against all suspected agents of suppression. In the heat of the struggle, the very presence of a white person in a gathering of Africans can bring scowls of resentment or possible violence. Now, there is a definite tendency toward forced racial identity even though individuals of all races differ radically among themselves in the realm of ideas.

Furthermore, missionaries often carry an actual share of the administrative responsibility of colonial governments. In Southern Rhodesia, the denominations administer the major part of the school system for Africans and, as such, are an "arm" of the government under the Ministry of African Education; just as this responsibility has been turned over almost exclusively to the Roman Catholic Church in both Angola and Mozambique.

The church frequently cooperates with the governments of Africa in medical and agricultural programs, as well as in educational ones, and this involvement is criticized increasingly. By accepting tax money as subsidies, even for benevolent purposes, the denominations leave themselves open to accusations of alignment with governments considered oppressive by the majority of the people. The day seems at hand when any sort of involvement with European-dominated governments—whatever the motives and goals of such relationships—is going to make the church suspect. As an acquaintance said to the author recently, "The drive for freedom is stronger even than that of economic well-being." Even if the church cooperates with minority governments to increase the physical well-being of the majority, the very recipients of that aid may still look upon the church-state relationship with suspicion and distrust.

Missionaries, because of their training and broad experience, are often placed in positions of administrative responsibility, and thus are identified with the government which administrates civil authority. In the minds of the masses, both the civil authorities and the missionaries are engaged in suppressive measures. Part of the positive drive toward freedom is the accompanying rebellion against established authority of any kind, and carries over into the life of the church as well as civic affairs.

The major blind spot of the total missionary program in Africa may well be the failure of European church leaders to foresee the approaching rebellion and to train nationals for administrative responsibility. Although some colonial governments have shown interest in educating the masses in central Africa, none have set about training Africans realistically for administrative responsibility under a democracy. There has been a failure to read the signs of the times. Too often there has been the erroneous idea that economic advancement would satisfy the African people—as if man ever lives by bread alone! Too often the denominations have followed government planning for, say, a fifty-year period of gradual turnover. Consequently there has been no urgency in helping Africans get the necessary training for administrative responsibility. Today's missionary is caught in the distasteful job of administration—he would like to drop it, but cannot because few Africans have been trained to take over. The modern missionary must bear the brunt of criticism and the stigma for the shortsightedness of his predecessors.

Some missionaries may be naïve enough to think that their African colleagues can carry responsibility without either training or experience; this may be kinder to believe than to think that they deliberately keep Africans from higher education. Some missionaries *have* blocked the way for capable Africans to proceed overseas. One observer of a local scholarship committee remarked, "Isn't it amazing how the capable boys are too bad to proceed for further training and the good boys are not smart enough?"

In all fairness, it should be stated that other missionaries have used their tithe and personal funds to help African young people get university training. Upon these few trained individuals the church depends for leadership during this time of crisis.

In *The Two Nations,* Richard Gray reports a conversation about education in Southern Rhodesia: ". . . the extremist viewpoint was put by Sir Hugh Williams, . . . 'If we could clear out every mission station in this country, and stop all this fostering of higher native education and development, we would much sooner become an asset to the Empire. . . . We are simply committing suicide.' "

Can it be that Portugal, with her long rule of over four hundred and fifty years in Africa, has had a similar fear of African advancement? How else can one account for the over ninety percent illiteracy rate of her African subjects? Within both the government and the church, the lack of adequately trained African personnel may be an excuse for retaining the administrative power in the hands of the European.

Perhaps the most serious problem, as seen by Africans, is the mutual position of privilege shared by colonial governments and missionaries. Too often the missionary, consciously or unconsciously, identifies himself with the government in order to preserve that position. This is an accusation that must be considered very carefully and objectively; it applies justly to some, not to others. But it must be faced.

Because missionaries came to Africa with more possessions, more education, and more experience than their African colleagues, they were often placed on pedestals. In many instances, they have made no move to step down. In specific actions and attitudes they have perpetuated their privileged status, and been aided and abetted by colonial administrators. Too often, both have shared a desire to perpetuate their common position as the "elite" of their society.

In many instances programs of church expansion and missionary activity have been motivated by an attitude of superiority. Every board of missions is aware that there is danger in sending to the mission field misfits in their own cultural backgrounds, who subconsciously feel that entering the mission field will give them opportunity to exert their own personalities over peoples less advanced. Fortunately this applies to few missionaries, but there *can* be a pseudo-missionary motivation arising out of a deep-seated feeling of inferiority and inability to meet competition in the homeland. Even the missionary who does not carry this attitude abroad finds it easy to bolster his ego by the ready-made position of privilege he finds upon his arrival. There is a desire to serve God; there is an intention to be obedient to the leading of God's Spirit; there is the hope of serving humanity; but there is also the enjoyment of serving in a situation where leadership is attained easily, quickly, and permanently. Many a young missionary-minister with little or no experience in the pastorate has been appointed a district superintendent at his first annual field conference.

Privilege is also seen in material possessions: large American-made cars, airplanes, larger residences, and home furnishings; in the assignment of administrative jobs, and in opportunities for the education of children.

Bishop Donal Raymond Lamont, of Umtali, Southern Rhodesia,

wrote in a recent pastoral epistle to his diocese (*Purchased People*), ". . . there could scarcely be two more violently contrasting systems of educational opportunity than those made available by the State to the European and those which apply to the African child. One has practically everything provided for him freely; the other must struggle and pay for the little that he has at all. A more thoroughly unjust state of affairs it would be difficult to imagine. . . ."

The privileged position of the missionary may also be seen in membership on decisive committees within the life of the church. For instance, of the twenty-three member denominations of the Southern Rhodesia Christian Conference, only one is headed by an African. The appointive power of the church is almost exclusively European.

The differential in salary for ministers maintains the position of privilege for the European. Probably the difference in educational qualifications fixes the position of privilege most firmly. Even in those denominations having ample democratic procedure and an African vote outnumbering the European, the lack of suitably qualified African candidates for high positions within the church often determines the choice of a European. In this way the church remains on a par with the government in maintaining European leadership.

2

Segregation

A CHARGE LEVELED against the Christian church in Africa is that it practices and promotes racial discrimination and segregation. There *is* enough of it to undermine the Christian witness throughout the continent—few, if any, churches have a clean record in this respect.

The African people are increasingly aware that what the sending church professes in theory, it may not always practice. In this age of instant news coverage, incidents of discrimination in Europe and America are quickly made known throughout Africa. Anti-integration riots in Alabama and Mississippi, the African students' protest in Bulgaria, the Little Rock crisis of a few years ago were all given prompt and detailed coverage in Africa, often with banner headlines. The sending churches seldom realize that their actions undergird or undermine Christian witness in Africa.

The discriminatory treatment given African students and diplomats in the missionaries' home countries probably causes the most negative reaction. If there are entrenched, discriminatory practices in the so-called enlightened and Christian countries of the world, what can one expect of their "ambassadors" sent overseas? If the church is ineffective in eliminating unjust practices in "Christian" countries, what can one expect on the frontiers?

Because they think that the leaders in the denominations twiddle their thumbs when they should be taking decisive action, the more impatient Africans are leaving the church and denouncing it; more may do so if the situation is not remedied. One must remember that Christianity is not the only option available to the religiously-minded man in Africa. Islam has the reputation of being a close, multiracial, religious fellowship. This, more than anything else, gives Islam an advantage over Christianity among animistic peoples of Africa. Just as in other parts of the world, people in Africa like the warmth of fellowship. If they cannot find true fellowship within the Christian church, they are going to look for it elsewhere. Today no one wants to come into the Christian church on a basis of inferiority; he either comes as an equal and enters into the warmth of fellowship, or he remains outside. Because the church has not adequately offered the hand of full fellowship to the African people, it stands severely judged.

A story, currently going the rounds, concerns the European who encountered an African emerging from a church. "Boy, what were you doing in that church?" the European asked brusquely.

The African, realizing the type of person speaking, replied, "Boss, I was just dusting the altar."

"That's all right, boy," said the European, "but don't ever let me catch you praying there!"

Even congregations which give generously toward the education and development of the African people may harm the cause of Christianity in Africa more than they help, if they themselves remain segregated and closed to nonwhites. No gift (whatever its size) will accomplish what is intended if the giver holds himself aloof from the recipient of his gift; for, " the gift without the giver is bare." No matter how much churches give of their substance to help the African people, if they practice segregation their gifts may be rejected as coming from the hand—not the heart.

It is customary to blame the Republic of South Africa for the most serious violation of the true Christian spirit because of their rigid apartheid. But the responsibility of the church in other areas cannot be lessened by trying to isolate the problem in one country only. In Southern Rhodesia, for instance, the Committee of Citizens Against the Colour Bar was resisted more by certain churches than by business and social establishments. In recent months many cinemas, hotels and restaurants have been declared multiracial, yet certain churches adamantly refuse the right of admission to non-Caucasians; others allow them to enter for worship but do little to make them welcome. There is also the

United States! Racial disturbances there are currently getting world-wide publicity. Shouldn't the Caucasian churches have supported this struggle for equality earlier? Had they done so, would presidential proclamations or congressional action be necessary?

Who can possibly calculate the insult which discriminatory practices have been to the African over the years? He is more sensitive today, when all the world is rocked by the struggle for freedom and equality, than ever before. The problem of segregation cannot be restricted just to the churches as institutions either. It is especially tragic in the lives of individual Christians in their relationships with Africans in day-to-day life. Writes one African schoolboy: "Missionary children are taught not to come in contact with Africans. They go to separate schools and yet there is an African school nearby. Thus, churches are the source of the colour bar; yet they preach that everyone is equal before God." Of course, the African ignores the fact that integrated schooling in his country is against the law—only recently has the law been repealed in regard to private schools—but were his school suddenly flooded with white students now, he would undoubtedly complain that so many Africans were being cheated out of an education! Nevertheless, his complaint has a basis in fact.

An African student in India commented ironically, "At your 'Christian' missions there are cemeteries where Christians must be buried when they die; most surprising is it that you even segregate dead bodies in your cemeteries. What is the meaning of this? This sort of thing destroys our faith in the church entirely."

It is important to understand how and why segregation came to be practiced. Much of this pattern of life developed unconsciously. The missionary tends to accept as his guide the cultural pattern of the country where he serves instead of seeking Christian principles in these matters. So many around him are seemingly adjusting to the established pattern that he scarcely knows he is conforming and, in conformity, failing to live a truly Christian life. One should remember Paul's instruction to his Roman friends, "Do not be conformed to this world but be transformed by the renewal of your mind that you may prove what is the will of God . . ." (ROMANS 12:2, RSV).

If a missionary comes from a cultural background in which racial discrimination is practiced, he is likely to accept the pattern even more naturally than those who have lived in nonsegregated societies. In any case, it is obviously much easier to fit into an established social pattern than to oppose it because of Christian principles.

When missionaries first arrived in Africa, they encountered a very underdeveloped people. One of three procedures became necessary from a practical standpoint: they could accept the standard of living; they could demand that the African people adjust immediately to the cultural pattern of the missionary group; they could simply keep the two cultures separate. In most instances, the missionary chose the third method. Later on, of course, the cultural gap between missionaries from the west and the African peoples gradually diminished; but the pattern of segregation remained. Unhappily, with most of the traditional reasons for the pattern disappearing, the habits of separation still prevail. The present cultural gap between European and African Christians is in general so narrow that close fellowship could be enjoyed were it not for the pattern of segregation which still exists. It is this pattern which today is limiting the effectiveness of the Christian witness throughout the African continent.

Again, the question of privileged position comes into play. Because the missionary is a member of the racial group which runs the colonial government, he has in times past found himself in an honored position merely by virtue of his pigmentation. The fact that his skin is white has often meant that he has had an elevated social position even before stepping onto the soil of his adopted land. The pattern of dominance of the white-skinned people has been undergirded and maintained by a false philosophy about the superiority of the ruling race. Tragic as it may be, it is not surprising that even churchmen have fallen into this pattern of thinking. There was a time, several decades ago, when anthropologists projected a theory that the Negroid peoples were different from Caucasians—both physiologically and psychologically—and that they would never develop beyond the mentality of a child. The French anthropologist, Levy-Bruhl, was the main proponent of this theory and it was accepted (consciously or subconsciously) by most of the governing nations as well as by some of the missionaries.

The demise of this theory of superiority of the Caucasian race can be brought about only by the granting of independence to all African people, thereby giving them the opportunity to develop their talents to the maximum.

In all fairness, this attitude of racial superiority was not encouraged in early days by the European colonists alone, but by the African peoples as well, who grew to consider themselves inferior. Treated as an inferior by the white man, the African was given little opportunity to prove that he was otherwise. In fact, often he did not try; he accepted the status; in earlier days he did not hear much about the concepts of freedom, equality, and dignity which are now so prevalent around the world.

But that day is past. The white man cannot use any "scientific" proof to support an assertion that the African is an inferior person. And Africans, at the same time, are demonstrating just how far and how quickly they can advance on all fronts—education, science, government, diplomacy, sports—when given the opportunity.

The church must reject categorically all attitudes and practices of racial superiority or inferiority if it is to make any positive impact upon present-day Africa. This is not just because Africans are going through a revolution in their own society; it is because they are *human beings*—full brothers in Jesus Christ. No human being has the right to relegate another to an inferior position on the basis of nationality, race, or cultural background. Unless all accept the idea of basic equality, the church in Africa may crumble and fall.

Recently, the author spoke to an interdenominational group of high-school pupils at the government Goromonzi Secondary School. After the address, during a discussion period, there were the usual questions focusing on the failure of the church to maintain a positive witness in the local social scene. Then a lad rose and said, "We are going to do away with the established churches in this country and then we shall build our own church based on the teaching of Christ."

There was wild applause.

3

Imperfect Missionaries

COUPLING THE WORDS "imperfect" and "missionary" may come as a shock to some. Many people assume that the ambassadors of Christ on the mission field are automatically issued a full complement of Christian qualities before they leave their homeland. Missionaries are people—and people are fallible and imperfect.

Anyone who knows the situation in Africa today knows also that western missionaries are being strongly criticized. Not only must they sustain the criticism directed against the church as a whole, but the more pointed censure directed against them as individuals as well.

It is, of course, impossible to live anywhere in this world without becoming the object of some criticism. Certainly all people who take stands on principles lay themselves open to criticism by those who may not agree with or understand them. The missionary has never been expected to please everyone (certainly it would be impossible to do so in this day), but oddly enough, he who tries to please everyone comes under the most violent attack, at the present time.

With the gap of misunderstanding widening between Africans and Europeans in those areas of Africa still under European domination, the missionary finds himself in an increasingly difficult position. It may be impossible for a sincere missionary to maintain a double loyalty—to the European community and the African one as well. Loyalty to one group already means almost automatic dissociation from the other. If the missionary is going to identify himself closely with the African people in their aspirations, he is going to lay himself open to more and more criticism from the European community—and vice versa. Racialism—be it black or white—is narrow and intolerant.

Young Africa *must* have its chance to criticize. Bitterness is evidenced by one high-school pupil who writes: "The attitude of some of the missionaries toward the African is atrocious. Some missionaries wouldn't allow any Africans to sit on their chairs or to ride in their cars. If you sit, they will spray where you have been sitting. Their children are advised not to come into contact with Africans."

A mature student now studying in India, and one who has had a great deal of association with missionaries from his early childhood onward, writes, "I dare say that many missionaries I have dealt with leave much to be desired about their earnestness of purpose in their church work. There is an undeclared emphasis on seeking a livelihood and perpetuating their position as bosses over the Africans."

A young man from an entirely different area in Africa, who is now studying in the States, comments, "Some missionaries refuse to promote Africans, saying that if they do so, they themselves will be forced to leave Africa."

Writes another, still in Africa, "My interpretation of the motivation of most missionaries is that of pitying the African and it seems to me that love is given the second position instead of emerging first."

The charges against individual missionaries are numerous; here are seven of the more serious ones: inability to communicate, unsympathetic attitude, lack of understanding, inability to produce results, failure to identify, lack of cooperation, and desire for segregation.

Some boards of missions have been tragically shortsighted in failing to insist that *all* missionaries master the language of the people with whom they are to work. In some churches eighty percent of the missionary personnel cannot communicate in the mother tongue of the people. In such instances the European language, understood imperfectly by many Africans and some missionaries, becomes a barrier to hurdle instead of an open channel for free communication. Although often it is not his fault, but the fault of his sending agency or the administration of his church, the missionary is blamed for his inability to communicate in the language of the masses.

Occasionally there are missionaries who just cannot communicate in *any* language. They have never learned the art of either logical thinking or public speaking. They go 'round and 'round in circles but never reach their goal. Fortunately their number is limited.

The unpopular missionary may have been sour before he left home or he may have become set against the world after leaving his native land. There may be reasons for his disappointments, but his unsympathetic attitude acts as a negative influence in the church. He has an adverse attitude toward his pupils, toward the church administration, toward all colleagues—be they African or European. An optimistic, positive, cheerful, sympathetic attitude is imperative if the missionary is to make a positive impact on the life of his associates.

Recently I heard of a missionary who created such a negative attitude on his mission center that pupils spat in the sand after he passed by. A cup of sour milk can turn the whole kettle.

Linked with the inability to communicate and an unsympathetic attitude toward associates is an indifference to local cultural values. Some missionaries feel that they have already learned all that is worth knowing, and with closed mind and rigid attitude they try to impart their superior knowledge to unreceptive ears. They assume that their own sets of values are unquestionably superior to any counter-set which they may find in others. They come only to teach—never to learn—and thus, close the door against opportunities to teach. He who refuses to learn soon ceases to have anything to share with others.

High-school pupils, in particular, complain that some of their missionary teachers are not qualified to teach the subjects to which they are assigned. So far, the church has sent few specialist-teachers to Africa; most are general missionaries. The specialist is hard to recruit and sometimes he finds conditions so different from those in his homeland that he becomes frustrated. Until recently, the general missionary has been qualified to give instruction in almost any subject taught in mission school. Now, with the rapid advance of education and the high standards set to pass established examinations, the day of the specialized teacher has dawned.

Often it is not the missionary who should be criticized but the sending board or committee which evaluated his ability, or the church administration on the field which forced him into an assignment for which both his superiors and he knew he was not prepared. Because of the pressing need, he has graciously tried to fill an existing gap—only to be criticized later on for trying to do so!

There was a time when the church agencies sending personnel overseas encouraged their young missionaries to identify themselves with the people of Africa. Apparently a change of attitude is taking place in the training centers of the U.S.A. and Europe, as today the fledgling seems to be advised *not* to identify too completely with his African colleagues. The main reason for this change in attitude appears to be to avoid emotional entanglements, especially between single young women missionaries and male Africans. Regardless of the reasons, any aloofness on the part of missionaries will decrease their effectiveness in whatever tasks they may be assigned.

There are all sorts of so-called valid reasons for the conservative attitude toward social mixing of the races. One of these is health. The assumption is that because of their local standard of living, African people are less hygienic than Europeans. If this be true, it is not due to any inherent difference between Africans and Europeans, but because lower economic groups in every society have less opportunity to practice good hygiene than do those living on a more privileged economic level.

Missionaries coming to Africa subject themselves to some health risks, but that is just an occupational hazard. Africans going to the States or to Europe must subject themselves to health hazards which do not exist in their own countries.

The missionary is subjected to temptations of pride, grudge-holding, jealousy, covetousness, impatience, and even physical lusts—all the temptations which taunt men everywhere. Some may feel that because they have answered the high calling as ambassadors for Christ, they no longer need check themselves regarding their attitudes and deeds. As one student in Europe wrote, "Some missionaries seem to think that the fact that they crossed the ocean means they are no longer subject to any temptation." (Perhaps the student had found that going to another continent had not made him perfect either?) No, crossing a body of water does not exempt anyone from the limitations of his human condition—no more so the missionary than any other man. Missionaries, above all people, should watch against the danger announced by Paul when he said, ". . . lest after preaching to others, I myself should be disqualified" (I CORINTHIANS 9:27, RSV).

Even when he acts with the best of motives and with clarity of purpose and purity of dedication, the missionary will be misunderstood. The fact that in a particular instance he may actually be "above reproach" does not mean that he is necessarily safe from *being reproached.* For there are people who (during this period of tension) deliberately seek to misunderstand—to discredit, and to misquote. There was a time when a missionary's action might have been given the benefit of the doubt. This is no longer true. Each missionary must realize that everything he does is being closely watched; he must be prepared to meet criticism honestly and calmly if he wants to make a positive witness in his ministry. Probably no people anywhere are under greater scrutiny than are the missionaries serving in Africa today.

An area in which a great deal of tension arises is that of education. If the missionary cannot understand the passionate desire of the African to liberate his mind and rise to a position of equality through education, he surely should not be in this part of the world at this time.

There is no more dominant motivation in the African community than this drive for education, unless it is the intense desire for independence. Basically, the two are coupled together. Missionaries are criticized because they do not see the importance of education in the development of this continent and of their particular church. There are those who would gladly relinquish all responsibility in education (even though the complete program would collapse), rather than share the arduous responsibility of trying to face the ever-increasing demands of the African people. Their reluctance to participate in an educational program or to encourage expansion in the field of education is often considered to be against African development.

However, even when missionaries are conscientiously working to extend educational opportunities, they are often misunderstood. In a country such as Southern Rhodesia (which supposedly has the most adequate educational facilities for African people of any country on the continent) there is constant pressure being brought to bear upon missionaries to force the government to offer more facilities more rapidly. The reason for this is clear and justifiable—there are many major bottlenecks in the facilities provided for Africans. In the church program of one denomination, there are one hundred and eighty-one lower primary schools, but only two high schools. There are over forty thousand students in this educational program. For this vast number of primary pupils, two high schools are pitifully inadequate. This means that there is a great loss of pupils between the last year of primary school and the beginning of high school. The missionaries in charge and the church directing their work are blamed for inadequate facilities.

Parents in Africa, as in all parts of the world, are anxious that their children get the best training possible. It is a terrible frustration to the African parent to have his child denied further educational opportunities at the beginning of high school. The missionaries are caught in the basic educational problem, for they have to interpret government regulations to parents. The missions cannot provide enough facilities with inadequate income from church and government sources, yet under a paternalistic system of government parents feel that they have a right to expect opportunities for educational advancement for their children. Parents know little or nothing about the efforts of churches on their behalf, and therefore blame the missionaries and the church authorities for not meeting the educational needs of the community.

In the face of such criticism, some missionaries become embittered and resentful; they feel the African shows a lack of proper gratitude for what the missions are doing. Regardless of the facts which motivate such a response, if missionaries let this negative attitude develop, they will hurt themselves, the church, and all with whom and for whom they work.

Unfortunate as it may be, there still appears to be some desire for segregation—even within the missionary force working in Africa. How else can one account for the missionary children sent hundreds of miles away from home to attend a strictly "white" school, ask critical young Africans, when an integrated one is within a few blocks? (It may be because of better-qualified teachers in the European schools, or better equipment, or stricter discipline, or simply conformity to an established social pattern.) Why are certain people always away from home when there is a nonracial conference? Can it be to avoid the embarrassment of entertaining African colleagues in their homes? (Here again social usage exerts a very strong influence. What might the neighbors say or think?) How can one account for the sharp and offensive remark heard recently from a first-term missionary who, in a weak moment, retorted, "If the Board wants us to entertain Africans, they should provide us with plastic coverings for our mattresses!"? How can one really account for the maneuvering of some missionaries to keep Africans out of places of key leadership within the African church? (The answer to this one is simple: most Africans have neither the training nor the experience for administrative responsibility.) Why then try to keep them from getting the training needed for responsible leadership? (Although answers also are given to this inquiry, they more often depict an attitude, than present a reason. They are usually highly paternalistic.)

Writes an African university student, "If Africa is to take her place under the sun—and this she must do—then she must exert her efforts through the leadership of her sons and daughters, whose self-reliance is long overdue. This is where the ruinous paternalism of missionaries comes into focus. It has become increasingly clear that the majority of these 'benevolent fathers' plan to remain permanently at the helm of affairs."

Yes, as a group, missionaries are not perfect. Neither the twenty-four-hour flight at an altitude of 33,000 feet nor the ten-day to three-week sea voyage can transform them into saints. Only God, through Christ, can do that. In his recent book, *No Saints Suddenly*, Bishop Hazen G. Werner has written, "No one becomes a saint suddenly any more than he becomes a well-read person suddenly. No one becomes indecent or dishonest suddenly any more than he becomes noble or dependable suddenly. You become what you have been thinking and doing a long time."

Although imperfect, most missionaries are "going on toward perfection," as John Wesley required of all his preachers. It is crucial to follow the injunction of Saint Paul: ". . . forgetting what lies behind and straining forward to what lies ahead, I press on toward the goal for the prize of the upward call of God in Christ Jesus" (PHILIPPIANS 3:13-14, RSV).

4

Limited Gospel

"*I KNOW THE WORK* of the Church is going forward," a young African acquaintance wrote the author not long ago, "but the rate of its forwardness is less than the rate of its backwardness." The phrasing of this comment may be amusing, but the indictment it makes, which is being made repeatedly against many churches throughout Africa, cannot be taken lightly. Unless the church takes cognizance of the rapidly changing continent—of what is happening—it may be completely bypassed and left as an ineffectual eddy along the main stream of life.

It is important to understand what the African people expect from their religion. John and Rena Karefa-Smart describe it in their book, *The Halting Kingdom*:

> The important thing in African religion is that every act of daily life has religious significance because through it one may either maintain good relations with the gods or offend them with possibly disastrous results. From sunrise to sunset, from birth till death, every act is under the scrutiny of the ancestors and of the gods and, therefore, is performed with due and proper regard to the correct form prescribed by experience as pleasing to the powers that control all of life.

If Christianity does not concern itself with *all* areas of life, it will ring a false note in the ears of sensitive Africans. What a priceless heritage—this sense of wholeness, oneness, the interrelatedness of life! For Christianity to fail to embrace all areas of life, as it proclaims its gospel, is a betrayal of its own authentic heritage and the best impulses of African religion.

The issue of the church's involvement in so-called secular

areas has always been one of debate among western peoples. At one extreme are those who counsel that the church "stick to religion" and not concern itself with wages, housing, politics, and other worldly matters. In contrast are those who are determined to plunge into any issue in the name of Christ. One can criticize either extreme; one can make the gospel narrow and ineffectual or so diffuse the influence of the church and bury it in social causes that it loses its force and identity as a Christian institution. In Africa right now the church seems more in danger of becoming disengaged to the point of irrelevance—of betrayal of its mission in the world—than of getting indiscriminately involved in all issues about it.

The western concept of a division between the sacred and the secular is difficult for the African to understand. He is often more mature than the westerner in this respect, for he sees life as a whole. He realizes that the sacred influences the secular while the converse is also true. He understands that the political development of his country will influence his freedom of worship. He knows also that if worship is to bring man into contact with God, it, in turn, should affect the political future of his country. Without acknowledging the source of his inspiration, an African high-school student wrote in an assigned theme:

> A religion true to its nature must also be concerned about man's social conditions. Religion deals with both earth and heaven, both time and eternity. Religion operates not only on the vertical plane but also on the horizontal. It seeks not only to integrate man with God but to integrate man with man and each with himself. . . . On the one hand it seeks to change the souls of men, and thereby unite them with conditions of man so that the soul will have a chance after it is changed. "Any church that professes to be concerned with the souls of men and is not concerned with the slums that damn them, the economic conditions that strangle them, and the social conditions that cripple them is a dry-as-dust church." (Used with permission of Dr. Martin Luther King.)

Some missionaries—because of a western concept of religion—have refrained from participation in all the activities of the community. By their example and their teaching they have often encouraged their followers to do likewise. In this time of turmoil in Africa, noninvolvement brings the missionary and the church he represents into disrepute. This is an affront to those educated Africans who are intensely aware of world events and who believe that there cannot be real freedom in other phases of life until political freedom has been achieved. A student writes succinctly, "An African of today needs a religion that is filled with universalism rather than particularism."

Another student: "The church must encourage youth to participate in politics as well as in church affairs. Once this is done, then we are sure of getting people who will be willing to apply the principles of Christianity as an instrument for getting their freedom rather than use violence. A good Christian enjoys politics."

Too often the western leaders of the church in Africa have discouraged active involvement in community affairs. Because many missionaries have alien residence permits only, they hesitate to take an active part in the affairs of a country in which they are not citizens. This attitude is not understood by some Africans who feel that missionaries tend to be "other worldly" about their social responsibilities. A student expresses this well when he protests, "I wish we could never hear such remarks as, 'We cannot interfere in political affairs because the government authorities made us sign agreements that we will never take an active part in politics.' Let everyone know that this is a very lame excuse to give for anyone who sees the right road to take, but for convenience chooses the easy path."

Another student comments, "Our church as a whole is afraid to enter the political venture of this country. I talked with a certain missionary who told me that he was afraid to criticize the government of this country because it would send him back home." Inactivity in the social-political struggle is often interpreted as lack of conviction and courage—looking after one's own interests rather than those of the Kingdom.

Not only have many churchmen refrained from political activity themselves, but they have counseled their church people to do likewise. On this point, little or no defense can be made. Because so many missionaries have taken this attitude, especially those of an older generation, many African pastors have accepted noninvolvement in community life as a basic Christian virtue!

What is taken for lack of involvement and unwarranted caution often is a sincere attempt on the part of missionaries and national church leaders to be objective in their approach to the social problems in Africa. Those who study the issues carefully, and as a result hesitate to act promptly, may be accused of twiddling their thumbs while emergency situations develop.

There is danger in being so objective and so fair—of trying to collect all the evidence, of attempting to wait until "all the facts are in"—one may find oneself totally out of touch with the swift turn of events around him. The picture of the "man of good will" standing and wringing his hands while history sweeps past him is a tragic one.

The church is in danger of rejection for exercising caution to the point of irrelevancy in the eyes of its politically conscious youth. It is this point for which the church has been most severely attacked. Whether the church as an organization should be a political force is open to serious question. Certainly it should not be partisan. But the involvement of the individual Christian, seeking to find solutions to his country's problems, is an obligation which the gospel places upon each believer. Religion and politics should not be divorced; to do so is to weaken and subvert both of them.

There is a time for the Christian to stand up and proclaim justice from the housetops, even though he knows his residence permit may be revoked. Some missionaries, after years of extreme caution in such matters, faced just such an issue in speaking up about conditions in Angola following the revolt in 1961. There is also a time to be silent; other missionaries have felt the more effective witness lies in remaining quiet and being allowed to continue at their posts. The committed Christian must be especially sensitive to the leading of God's Spirit to know which course to take at a given time.

Some conscientious Christians believe that it is best to work quietly and constantly behind the scenes—in expectation of a gradual improvement of conditions—instead of becoming openly involved in the struggle. However good this kind of service may be (and it *does* take courage to be steadfast), when the issues are clear the African Christians expect their church leaders to stand up and be counted.

Youth feels that older Christians are more interested in reading their Bibles, singing, and praying than in struggling to attain stature and dignity as mature world citizens. Probably they are. As individuals grow older, they tend to become more conservative. The question of the Christian's relationship to his environment is most worrisome to the older generation, and understandably so. Many critical Africans understand this problem in its proper perspective; recently one of them wrote, "We know that it is rather difficult for the older missionaries because the rate at which this country is changing is too great for them. This also applies to our older African people." It is youth who welcomes change and who can keep up with the accelerated pace at which changes are being made throughout the continent.

The gospel makes its full impact only when the individual who has been personally redeemed goes out into society to make his witness in all areas of life. Recently a missionary told the author that his job as a school administrator made it impossible for him to witness to his faith. He said he was so involved in routine matters of education that he had no time to witness. Surely the most effective witness is made *in* rather than apart from the interrelated tasks of life! Many of the most effective Christians are those who speak rarely *and* briefly, but whose every act bespeaks the love of Christ.

5

Culture

AS ONE WALKS or drives along the streets of Salisbury, Southern Rhodesia, he may well see Africans wearing hats made of the skins of various animals. These hats were associated with the now-banned Zimbabwe African People's Union and have become a badge of sympathy with the movement for African political independence. The African wearing the fur hat may have on a very up-to-date western suit; but the hat is a defiant assertion that he is no longer willing to abandon the age-old ways of his own people. The hat is the symbol of an emerging consciousness of values in the indigenous African culture; it implies a growing suspicion that no longer is everything western to be embraced and everything authentically African to be deprecated.

For many years, anthropologists have criticized missionaries for destroying African culture. Much of that criticism has been heard and disregarded, for the desire of many anthropologists was to preserve Africa as a museum piece. This would mean the withdrawal not only of missionaries but of all other agents of acculturation. This should *not* be done. Cultural exchange should and will go on throughout the world, but it must be an exchange on the basis of merit. No people can truly come into a position of maturity and responsibility without a sense of continuity with their own past and respect for the value of their own attainments.

There have been some anthropologists, however, who have been interested in the *people* of Africa, not as museum pieces, but as individuals who needed some ties with the past to give them security to face the current winds of change. Now the African people themselves are joining in the chorus of criticism against the European in general and the unpopular missionary in particular, for robbing them of their cultural heritage.

Currently the pendulum is swinging away from the use of European customs. Not long ago I attended the annual Youth Fellowship retreat of some fifty high-school students and teachers. Through an oversight, I had not received the full set of delegate instructions, and was therefore embarrassed to discover I had no utensils for my noonday meal! Someone rose to the occasion and handed me a plate laden with heaping portions of sadza (heavy corn meal mush), meat, and muriwo (collards, cabbage, or some other greens cooked with the meat). Helplessly I looked around for a fork or spoon; those near me had already begun to eat, and apparently didn't notice my predicament. With a twinkle in her eye, a teen-age girl (a student at Hartzell Teacher Training College) asked why I wasn't eating.

"I'm afraid I forgot my tools," I replied.

"Use your fingers!" she laughed. Just then someone handed me a fork, and I fell to. As I ate I noticed that several other delegates in my predicament, had not waited for her advice—they were unself-consciously and deftly fingering the remains of the meal into their mouths. "Why not?" I am sure they reasoned— an African hostess always passes a basin of warm water and a towel before a meal, and again at its close.

The first missionaries arrived with the colonizers, and knew little of African culture. Most assumed that nothing in Africa was comparable to that of the west. Without trying to analyze or evaluate the African culture, they presumed that almost everything African was evil—to be denounced and destroyed, if possible. As a result, some missionaries patterned their way of life as closely to the western model as possible. Their premise was that the African should leave his "heathen ways" and move into "civilized" ways when he accepted Christianity.

"I believe the early missionary rather confused Christianity with the western way of life," wrote an African university student. This was the understatement of his long essay. The European has often failed to separate certain phases of his culture from the essence of Christianity. The vacuum cleaner, the hot-water bottle, the big car with high gasoline consumption, the cake mix and the ice cream powder, the umbrella and the galoshes, the refrigerator and the hi-fi, the bread slicer and the potato peeler—what do these and hundreds of other gadgets have to do with Christianity?

Kneeling may not be the most worshipful position for prayer. Standing may not be a gesture of respect when the schoolteacher enters the room—prostration before the chief was the sign of respect in many African tribes. Letting the lady go first might expose her to danger; for this and other reasons, in African society the women usually followed their husbands. Is it more Christian for a housewife to give thanks when she puts the food on the table instead of when she pours the cassava flour into the boiling water in her clay pot? Is it more Christian to look another straight in the eye than to avoid the direct glance? Is there anything holy about the heavy sacramental vestments worn in a cold climate or the clerical garb so unsuited for the tropics? Is there anything sanitary or especially Christian about shaking hands? Why should the delightful, ceremonial, handclapping greeting be discarded? Is baker's bread more suitable for the communion table than a kernel of soft corn or a slice of plantain? Is wine more symbolic than African sweet beer?

Most early missionaries learned African languages. A number of anthropological monographs attest to the fact that some missionaries were not totally without appreciation of African culture. Books such as *The Ila-Speaking People of Northern Rhodesia* by the Reverend Edwin W. Smith and Captain Andrew Murray Dale and Henri Junod's *The Life of a South African Tribe* indicate that the missionary community has at times appreciated African culture, not only from an anthropological viewpoint, but from a religious one as well. Some of the early missionaries, and even a few in Africa at the present time, have failed to appreciate the indigenous African culture and in various ways have helped to destroy it.

Following the pattern set by early missionaries, African pastors, evangelists, and Bible women often accepted the missionary attitude that everything western was to be embraced and everything African discarded. They were careful to follow in the steps of their western mentors—too often this meant that the good news of western culture was proclaimed instead of the Good News of Jesus Christ. This pattern has been followed so extensively, for such a long period, that much of the value of African culture is lost—or on the verge of being lost—to the church. In some churches this process of rejection of African culture and assumption of western ways has gone to such an extent that there are Africans who have "outwesterned" the westerners themselves. They have long since adjusted to certain patterns of western culture and the older group especially have no intention of looking back to try to pick up valuable elements from their own culture. For them, unfortunately, those elements are gone forever.

Professor E. B. Castle describes this graphically in "Adverse Conditions in Childhood":

> The old type of moral instruction given by grandparents and mothers by means of proverbs, folk stories and myths, is disappearing because Christian teaching condemns them as pagan and sinful. Thus the conflict between a misinterpreted Christianity and traditional beliefs ends in a shelving of responsibility by parents; and into this quicksand the African child is born. Schools and Christianity, say some of the old people, have undermined customary discipline. Christian morality, so complex and in so many ways in conflict with tribal tradition, is now regarded as superior because the white man is superior in his knowledge and power. Hence moral instruction is left to schools and the parents abdicate from a task which they now find beyond their capacity.

Among the younger Africans, another attitude is emerging. They have studied world history and realize that all people have contributions to make out of their own cultural backgrounds. There is a definite turning to the past—a searching in the ashes for elements which have been resistant enough to survive the fires of westernization—in the hope that something truly African can be found. It is exciting to see people rediscover things which are their own and cease borrowing indiscriminately from other cultures. Their most difficult task is to convince their own parents and others of the older generation that some aspects of their culture are of value. From India an African university student writes:

At my home school, where I was a teacher and its headmaster, I was surprised and sorry to find that parents there, including my own, discouraged the use of the drum to accompany singing. The reason given was because the drum was used to accompany songs of tribal worship in the past, therefore it must go; it is heathen in this Christian era! I consider it a shameful loss to let the African drum go out of use on the African scene. They hated the slightest sound of a drum, even on wedding days. I cannot think of a more suitable musical instrument for such occasions!

Equally fantastic was the changing of names at the time of baptism. Why should such beautiful names as Chipo, Nyasha, Chuma, Tendai, Kudzai, etc. be replaced with such names as Draper, Gift, Grace, Smart, Washington, Maxwell, etc.? While there is nothing wrong with such English names, one really finds no sufficient reason to substitute them for the meaningful African names. I find nothing unchristian in them. . . . I fear that the use of foreign names tends to alienate Christianity and thus stops it from anchoring its roots in the soil of the land. In addition, it helps to perpetuate the existing feeling of superiority on the part of one race, and of inferiority on the part of the other.

Along with names, our folklore is fast going out of use. Our beautiful nganos, zvisanas, zviparis (tales, idioms, and proverbs); our songs and lullabys; our rural arts and crafts like reed-mat-making, fibre-mat-making, pottery; song-making; peanut-butter-making; our dances; basket-making, etc. have in some places almost vanished. Our languages seem to be losing their taste among educated people and, unless we are careful, they may be swallowed up by English. This would be a great loss. Among the many factors influencing this degeneration of African culture, to my mind, is that missionaries and white men as a whole were prepossessed by the unfortunate appellation "Dark Continent" of Dr. David Livingstone so that they failed to see or to seek to improve this civilization in the African culture. Through this misnomer, their approach was more or less the process of elimination by substitution.

Our local vegetables like derere, guku, musungusungu, muboora, mbowa, chowa, runhi, etc. are looked upon as primitive in the eyes of cabbages, turnips, spinach, and their like! Our local fruits like mazhanje, hute, shakata, mavonde, hubva, nhenzvera, maroro, matunduru, matohve, matamba, mawugy, nhengeni, etc. have almost been replaced by plums, apricots, apples, dates, etc.—at least in the houses of those who consider themselves civilised and educated. Our staple grains of maize, rapoko, mhunga, and mapfunde are giving way to rice and oats. Our earthen water pots are giving way to buckets despite the fact that buckets make the water rusty by oxidation; our traditional drink of sweet beer (not intoxicating) has almost completely yielded to tea and coffee. It is sad to relate that while we have forsaken these rich things in themselves, we find ourselves falling short of reaching for the "civilised" things we aspire to, as the salaries we receive unfortunately don't warrant our affording these imported things; so we starve or lack good nutrition in a land of plenty!—much to the malicious joy of the white man.

Some members of the younger generation are becoming quite vocal in their resentment against those who have sought to destroy their cultural heritage. This does not imply that they do not recognize the values which the west has brought to them, the continuing contribution which western culture can still make to Africa—but they are not willing to accept the old assumption that just because something can be called "western" it is inherently more valuable than the indigenous culture of Africa.

This bitterness is reflected in a letter written by an African student now overseas: "The church sought to ruin the practice of our traditions and interfered with our sacred things and introduced their own God in place of our God who would listen to us. Hence, we are now at the white man's mercy because we have lost our God. They have demoralized the African and today they can do anything with us." Naïve as this may seem, the force of the criticism is strong, and the basic point made must be considered seriously.

Three of the areas most severely criticized are medicine, personality, and music (and the relationship of the latter to worship). One of the worst effects of the European superiority attitude has been the curtailment, if not outright elimination, of the practices of African herbalists. No one knows just how valid this practice was in precolonial days; many Europeans considered it simply superstition and magic. But now there's a growing feeling that the African herbalists were the scientists of their day, and that they discovered many herbs which were effective medicine and which have since been lost. That the African people have survived in their tropical climate, with its myriad germ-carrying insects, is a tribute to so-called primitive herbalists. It is tragic that much of the knowledge of the herbalists has been overlooked or forgotten. It will be unfortunate for African society as well as for world culture if the lore of the herbalists is not recaptured and preserved. Undoubtedly some of their practice *was* based on superstition and magic; but there was enough scientific knowledge to merit preservation of their work.

The African personality is most attractive: gracious, thoughtful, confident, dignified, and winsome. There is an African way of doing things. Some things should be done deliberately, sensitively, and rhythmically; some things demand caution while other things should be undertaken with abandon and enthusiasm. What a pity that some of these codes of conduct are on the verge of being lost!

Writes an observing student, "While the African adopted new names and acquired new skills and a new way of life, he parted with some of his precious inherent traditions which were part and parcel of his being. Our children no longer respect the African code of behaviour because the church tells them our traditions are heathen. If losing some of our good qualities and skills was a condition in the contract of receiving the white man's civilisation, it was a costly one."

With the African's understanding that religion is something permeating all life and controlling all actions, it is only natural that he should look to the church leaders with hurt in his eyes and sharp accusation in his voice.

There is a similar problem in regard to the church's treatment of African music. Most of the traditional music with its rhythm and drumbeat has been replaced by western music. This was illustrated most forcefully when an African choir traveled two hundred miles to present a concert to an African congregation. They sang some twenty-five different numbers, not one of which was authentic African music! Most of the congregation saw nothing wrong with the procedure—some of those responsible for the choir even expressed astonishment when the question was raised. "Those hymns and anthems *are* African! They were sung in Shona—not in English!" The church has made its service, its ritual, and its music conform to a foreign pattern and as a result it has created two attitudes among Africans. One group feels there is no other way to have a church; those individuals have been thoroughly conditioned. The second group feels that the church is not theirs at all; it belongs to the Europeans.

In *African Music and the Church in Africa*, Henry Weman, who has done tremendous research on the subject of African music, says,

> A cursory contact with music in Africa provides ample evidence that there is something wrong with the educated African's attitude to music. There is no doubt that in school and in church he does his best to sing the stipulated tunes, but since these are—almost without exception—European, it is seldom that a song succeeds in loosening his tongue. He is moving in an alien world, and if his heart fails to beat in time with the music, that is only to be expected.

Until one has heard Africans singing their own folk music, one might be satisfied with the way they sing western church music, for they do about as well with it as do westerners themselves. Says Weman,

> Without doubt, the Church has acted in good faith in attempting to bring to life in the Christian congregation that musical heritage which has proved itself to be such a vital factor in public worship within western Christendom. But when experience has shown African and western music to be two distinct entities, both church and school ought to recognize African music, and give it a chance to prove itself by the side of imported music. . . . An alien musical language can never become the spontaneous expression of man's innermost desires and feelings. A service of worship can hardly be the true expression of devotion, praise, and prayer if its forms of expression are foreign.

When the forms of expression are his own, "music mirrors the soul of the African and is an essential part of his inmost being;

it has the power to liberate and it is in the music and the dance that the African can best be himself," Weman adds.

Words of a young African Christian call the church to self-examination once again: "If the missionaries, in addition to teaching staff notation and tonic sol-fa, had taught us to improve our mbiras, drums, flutes, and other instruments and to perfect our traditional music and dances, what a rich culture we would have by now!"

One reason the church is losing people is because it has failed to capture them emotionally through westernized forms of worship. The great Wesley hymns and those of Watts and others have profound meaning for the British and Americans; Negro spirituals have special meaning for Americans. Neither European hymns nor spirituals have real emotional meaning for Africans, for they came from neither personal experience nor their own culture.

When a westerner looks into history, he discovers that the use of indigenous tunes (to which Christian words were fitted) gave the Wesleyan revival in England acceptance among the masses. Yet, this principle is not recognized in the church in Africa. "West is best!" seems to be an assumption underlying many things.

Painful as it is to admit that the church has been an agent of destruction of African culture, in all fairness one cannot but agree with the student who claims that "many Christians think that they are in Africa to impose their western culture without first finding out what good the people already have." And, as the present swinging back to traditional African customs gains momentum, the church will suffer for having identified itself more with western culture than with the gospel of Jesus Christ. The words of another student call the church to a new role: "I am not against adopting the new ways of life in acquiring better culture, but I am only suggesting that such importations would be more useful, meaningful, and stronger if cemented with the best of our customs and traditions. If the new skills and new ways of life could have been additions and not wholesale substitutions for the local patterns of life, we should be a lot richer today."

The God revealed in Jesus Christ cannot be identified so narrowly with one particular culture or way of doing things. To deny the African's respect for and cultivation of the values of his indigenous culture is to betray fundamental principles of the Christian tradition. Certainly the great God of us all is more interested in the salvation of people than in the preservation of western culture.

6

Hypocrisy

TO UNDERSTAND AFRICA or the African people one must grasp the basic concept of the wholeness of life: all phases of life merge into one stream which gives man his personality, attitudes, and values. Man acts as he does because of his set of values—in short, because of his religion. A man's religion is not something to be seen on given occasions and in prearranged settings; it is that part of man which reflects God's image and motivates him in all actions; it guides him in his value judgments.

In most parts of southern Africa, the majority of the people know something of New Testament teaching. The life of Jesus is taught in most schools, beginning in kindergarten. The values which controlled Jesus' life are generally known and appreciated.

Most Europeans living in Africa are at least nominally identified with the church; they usually attend services on Christmas or Easter, if not both. They turn to the church for the great festive and transitory occasions of life: baptism, marriage, burial. They come from the so-called Christian countries to settle in Africa. Their culture has been influenced by Christianity. They call themselves Christian and are so labeled by others. These lay people, together with the missionaries, represent the church wherever they go and whatever they do.

It is only natural that there is considerable confusion in the mind of the unsophisticated African as he compares and contrasts the average imperfect Christian with the ideal taught and lived by Jesus. His logical conclusion is that Christianity is either powerless in its motivation or that the so-called Christians are deliberately obstructing that power in their lives. One thing is certain: the gap between the ideal and the real is so great as to indicate insincerity of purpose. Many are asking with this student: "If Christianity calls for love, why is it that some of the white people don't show it in their treatment of the Africans?"

The only answer is, "They don't believe the gospel or they would act as Jesus did." In Africa, as in Europe, America or the Orient, many look at the church and shout "hypocrisy!"

We *must* look at some of these accusations: the little inconsistencies, the evident discrepancies, and basic dishonesties.

All people are inconsistent at times without meaning to be so. One may be preoccupied and his preoccupation may be interpreted as a slight. On Sunday one may recognize someone in church because he expects to find him there, but on Wednesday when he meets him on the street, he may not recognize him; he may, in fact, be thinking of some problem and not really see *him* at all.

A high-school pupil complained, "The weakness of the church is due to the fact that the missionaries preach in church, telling people to love their neighbours but they themselves do not love their neighbours. The missionary school man is good only when he is at school. If you meet him in town, he shows you his true colours and does not recognize you."

Another student said, "At an African's funeral, very few missionaries are present; but, if it is a white person's funeral, they all come. This makes the Africans think that the missionaries are hypocrites."

Absence from a funeral in Africa, when attendance is possible, indicates an estrangement from the deceased. The missionary's sense of obligation to his assigned task may be interpreted as a lack of affection for a beloved member of the community.

Africa is still a continent of pioneer countries, as far as the majority of the Europeans are concerned. Isolation from other Europeans and separation from family controls often give a feeling of license, a certain laxness in morals. The monogamous ideal, as proclaimed by Jesus, has not always been followed by Europeans in Africa.

Some of the early Portuguese settlements in Angola were colonized by convicts sent from Portugal—deported rather than put in prison. Their moral standards in Angola were no different from what they had been in Portugal. However, not only ex-convicts cohabited freely with African women; so did the early traders and government officials. It is widely rumored that some representatives of the church did not always maintain their vows of celibacy and chastity; if these rumors are true, the church has accommodated itself in practice to a pattern of life which it officially repudiates. Until European women began coming to Africa in fairly large numbers, it was not unusual for a white man to maintain two families—a white one in Europe and a colored one in Africa. Socially, this was condoned and (reportedly) not even frowned upon by the church, so long as the mulatto children were baptized and cared for.

In other parts of Africa there has been much less miscegenation than in Portuguese areas of influence; but marital fidelity has not been especially high. Southern Rhodesia has a very high divorce rate, along with a high liquor consumption, and consequently a tragically high rate of motor-car accidents. Isolation alone cannot take the blame, of course; intoxication and the increasing number of broken homes in European and American society testify to a widespread decline in adherence to Christian principles.

Unfortunately, many educated Africans—seeing these actions by the so-called Christians—feel that monogamy is only a white man's screen for sexual licentiousness. Some say cynically, "The white man has several wives, too; he has them one at a time, disposing of them as he tires of them." Many Africans believe that fidelity within a polygamous system is far superior to organized prostitution or monogamous infidelity.

One of the highest values in the traditional African tribal life was "the common good"—practiced within certain restricted limits, to be sure. However, the idea of fellowship and brotherliness as preached and practiced by Jesus was not an entirely new notion, except in its inclusiveness. The ideal of the common good has been a motivating force for centuries in Africa and was at the very heart of religion. It is, therefore, with a certain amount of disdain that the African people witness the lack of brotherliness among European Christians as well as toward other nationalities and races.

One of the early setbacks for the Christian church in Africa south of the Sahara was the involvement of Europeans, including some missionaries, in slave trading along the west coast. In *The Planting of Christianity in Africa*, C. P. Groves claimed:

> The active pursuit of the slave-trade accompanied the Christian mission and was not thought amiss. Indeed, the very mission possessed slaves of its own; a Jesuit monastery at Loanda was endowed with 12,000. When the slave-trade was developed between Angola and Brazil, the bishop of Loanda, on a chair of stone by the quayside, bestowed his episcopal blessing on the departing cargoes, promising them future felicity when the stormy trials of life were over. Father Barroso was a spokesman for those who later acutely felt the shame of it, and saw in the condonation of the traffic a major cause of ultimate missionary failure.

Recently, a historical chapel down by the Luanda harbor was declared a national museum. Through there in olden days the slaves were driven to ships for transportation to the new world. It is reported that, as they passed a certain point, a representative of the church sprinkled holy water on them so that in case they did not survive the rigors of the ocean trip, their souls would find their way to purgatory and—perchance—to heaven.

Those were unenlightened days and allowances must be made for that fact. Unfortunately, the lesson of the Good Samaritan has still not been learned by some; and this willful ignorance gives rise to some of the impotence of the church in Africa.

This very demand of the gospel is one reason why it is so hard to be a Christian in Africa; there are so many truly needy people that if he is sensitive to the needs of others one is constantly bled limp. There is such a constant call for outgoing love and resources that the practicing Christian needs intervals of retreat to the mountains for rehabilitation, revitalization, and renewal— and to the bank to discuss his overdraft!

A few weeks ago, the author was discussing with a missionary the question of picking up African hitchhikers as he speeds rapidly to town. His justification for his lack of samaritanism was, "But I wouldn't do that even in America!"—as if the American cultural pattern determines what is Christian! Another missionary with whom the author discussed the same question replied, in astonishment, "But, my car is my castle!"—but do not even kings view their subjects compassionately? So often the European looks down from his castle and supposes that the common man is happy as he trudges his weary, endless miles to the store to buy a box of matches or a kilo of sugar. One dear missionary (may her tribe increase!) never passes a pedestrian but what she calls out, *"Nda guta!"* ("I'm completely full"); they know that she is referring to the car and not herself! For those who are accustomed to rushing from one place to another in cars, it makes little difference whether or not they stop and pick up pedestrians; but to those who walk, it may suggest the difference between being a real Christian and a phony.

A few months ago, Africans sat for the first time in the Southern Rhodesian Parliament. One of the first actions of the opposition was a motion to eliminate by law any discriminatory limitations for the members of Parliament. The motion was defeated. Thus, in a so-called Christian society, duly elected members of Parliament voted down a motion to extend everyday courtesies and rights to a minority of its own members! What kind of Christian brotherhood is this?

Those from afar need not smack their lips with self-righteousness. A distinguished friend of mine was asked to leave a Sunday morning service of worship in the USA because his skin happened to be a little darker than that of other worshipers. Is it any wonder that Christians are accused of saying one thing and doing another, thus revealing their insincerity and hypocrisy? Is it any wonder that average people raise their eyebrows in disbelief when they hear colonial governments say that they can't possibly expend larger sums on African education, while at the same time they treble the amount spent for national defense to suppress by force the growing demands for independence? Let it be remembered that those in power who are responsible for such unbrotherly acts are usually lay representatives of the church. The Europeans themselves may not think that they ought to be so labeled; but surely they would not want to be called unchristian, pagan, or heathen!

People in Africa know little about the waste and extravagance among fellow Christians abroad, especially in America. But they do know something of it. They see it in American movies; they read of it in their papers; they hear it spoken of by their fellow men who have traveled overseas. They see it to a lesser degree in the unpopular missionary. And, in time, they will probably see it exemplified in their own leaders!

"Get all you can; save all you can; give all you can," was John Wesley's admonition. Today, many Christians are glad enough to follow the first part of that advice; most are happy to abide by the second; but not so many remember the third part. Or, if they do, they greatly underestimate the word "can" when it applies to their giving. John Wesley meant, by that advice, to establish a pattern of simple living. He did not envision that there would ever be wealthy Christians. How could there be when they would be giving so much? What a tragedy that his followers haven't followed the example of the simple life, as first set by Christ Himself! Daniel Fleming wrote in *Living as Comrades*:

A Christian movement which does not come to grips with the problem of attaining justice for all will not seem relevant to the dominant world conditions of our time. Christian leaders are beginning to feel this so deeply that they are questioning whether evangelistic efforts for the masses will be really dynamic and decisive, whether evangelism in any land will be taken seriously, unless Christians everywhere find some way of divorcing the Christian message from the luxury and materialism which typify our western culture. In a world where the demand for social and economic justice is being pressed as never before, the masses may take notice of the Christian message only when Christians themselves find a new way of living, possibly a drastically new way, which demonstrates their concern over a world half-prosperous and half-slum.

Until Christians begin to show more love and neighborliness, they are going to have to support the accusation of hypocrisy in their religious practices and see the church limp along in only partial fulfillment of its high calling. To quote Dr. Fleming again, "This matter of justice raises a deep spiritual issue, so that the problem of simplification in living becomes a concern for every sincere Christian wherever he lives in the world."

Finally, there is a basic dishonesty practiced by some Europeans in Africa. In a land where many people interpret the law as they wish, anything can and does happen. One need not have the eyes of a hawk to see irregularities practiced against defenseless people in rural Africa. A finger on the scales, bent-in measuring tins, the move of the marking finger before cutting yard cloth, a shortage in change, and a dozen other things are all tricks of the trade. They can be practiced by anyone who is dishonest, but the tragic thing is that so often they have been engaged in by Europeans in their dealings with Africans. Little wonder that some Africans are skeptical of some of the religious values held by Europeans—they shrink, as do his weights and measures!

Land has great value for the African; without a piece of land, he feels insecure. It is probably the seizure of land by the European which has alienated the African from him and his religion as much as anything else. A popular saying about the early missionary movement in Africa went, "When the first missionaries arrived, they had the Bible and the people had the land. Now the Africans have the Bible and the Europeans have the land." This cynicism is too close to truth to be ignored.

Over and over again the author has seen the coffee gardens of Africans in the north central part of Angola taken over by Europeans. It is usually done legally—but not harmlessly. The European "finds" coffee trees growing "wild" in the forests. He notes the location and marks out his own plantation to include the coffee gardens of several Africans. Notices are posted in Luanda, two hundred miles away, and perhaps in the European-language newspapers. A notice may even be posted on the local administration bulletin board. Even if he is aware of what is happening and is interested in protesting, the African knows that he has little more than one chance in ten of winning any expensive legal case; so he remains quiet, and when the European moves in, the African farmer resignedly marks out another coffee garden for himself—in a deeper forest. But there is always a time of reckoning and that time has already come to Angola.

The Right Reverend Donal Raymond Lamont, Roman Catholic Bishop of Umtali, Southern Rhodesia, raises a question regarding the estrangement of Africans from land in Southern Rhodesia. In his Pastoral Instruction entitled "Purchased People," he writes, ". . . although it is frequently stated that the Land Apportionment Act was introduced to protect the African and to prevent his being rendered completely landless, there must surely exist in many minds, doubts about the honesty of acquiring so much land so easily from a primitive and unsuspecting people."

For those interested in Christ's church, the tragedy lies not only in those who have died in the war in northern Angola, or the landless ones of Southern Rhodesia or Kenya, but that the church has been so weak that it cannot condition its adherents to follow a way of love. It is only as the gap between the ideal proclaimed by Jesus and the way of life followed by His modern disciples narrows that the Christian witness becomes effective. The *theory* of brotherhood will not remove the stigma of hypocrisy attached to the church; but actual *living* together as brothers will go a long way towards doing so.

7

Division

THERE ARE MANY Christians of all communions who long
for that unity which Jesus Christ willed. "There is no longer
room or justification in Africa for tribal or colonial or racial
churches," wrote Dr. John Karefa-Smart in *The Halting Kingdom.* Should he have added that there is no room for denominational divisions? Many Africans, especially those actively
engaged in denominational church work, feel that the barriers
which divide should be broken down.

In the summer of 1959 the author gave a series of lectures at
the Ricatla Union Seminary in Mozambique. There were students from at least four denominations attending the institution
at that time. In the discussions following the lectures, it was
agreed that one of the weaknesses of the church in Africa is its
divisive nature. As yet not all are united in one body even
though all may recognize Christ as their common Head.

It may be well to give briefly a picture of the Christian divisions in Africa. First of all one is very conscious of the wide
division between Roman Catholic and Protestant groups, especially in those areas under the influence of the southern European countries. The Catholic-Protestant feeling is so strong,
especially in Mozambique and Angola, that a few years ago the
late Cardinal Gouveia (the only Roman Catholic Cardinal in
Africa at that time) issued an Easter pastoral letter in which he
listed Protestantism as one of the three major enemies of the
state.

In countries where there is a predominant Roman Catholic
influence, Protestant missions have often entered into comity

agreements whereby no two denominations would work in the same geographical or linguistic area. The practical reasons for this are seen at once. Where languages have to be learned and literature prepared, it is better to concentrate. Also, Roman Catholic officials cannot understand competition among Protestants and, in general, have discouraged Protestant denominational overlapping. Some more pietistic and individualistic groups have not always entered into or adhered to comity plans, but as a rule there has been general cooperation on the matter.

In predominantly Protestant countries, namely those under the spheres of British influence and in Liberia, there have been fewer comity agreements and consequently more denominational confusion. The apex of denominational overlapping is found in the Republic of South Africa where there are more than a thousand Protestant denominations and sects, some of the latter with only a few score adherents. Separatist churches are growing in number in Southern Rhodesia where there are already approximately seventy different groups, and in other parts of the continent as well. It is embarrassing for me to admit that probably in no other part of the world, outside of the United States, are there as many Methodist groups competing with one another as in Southern Rhodesia and Mozambique. Almost all of them are related to the World Methodist Council. In Mozambique the African Methodist Episcopal, the Free Methodist, and *The* Methodist Church (all with home bases in the United States), plus the Methodist Church of South Africa, are engaged in evangelistic efforts. In Southern Rhodesia the grouping is about the same, except that the Methodists from the United Kingdom replace those from South Africa. In addition there are at least three separatist Methodist churches operating in Southern Rhodesia. It is quite evident that considerable confusion must exist when discussing church affiliation among the unenlightened. For a Methodist to further differentiate whether he is "Free," "American," "United Kingdom," "African Episcopal," "Independent," or just "African" is no small task, especially when traditions, doctrines, and practices are quite similar.

The people in Africa have traditionally been divided among hundreds of tribes and even subdivided into clans and families.

Thus there had been strong group loyalties which held people together either in limited communities or extending over wide areas. Then the church came in and redivided the African people along religious lines, with Moslems claiming a large share of converts especially in the northern, western, and eastern parts of the continent.

As a young missionary, I did not fully appreciate the negative reaction of some local chiefs to the evangelistic efforts of the churches. (At that time it was usually just the Protestants and Roman Catholics who competed for the loyalty of the villagers.) A convert to either religion usually moved out of the chief's village and started a subvillage of his own. This was considered a wise practice so that Christians could support and encourage each other in a better way. The common pattern was a Protestant subvillage, the chief's main village, a Roman Catholic subvillage, and perhaps a Seventh Day Adventist subvillage. The chief may or may not have exercised full control over all segments of his village; as often as not, the catechist (evangelist or class leader) preempted the prerogatives of the chief over his own adherents.

The Reverend Ndabaningi Sithole wrote in *African Nationalism,* "In many places tribal consciousness is being pushed into the background, and Christian consciousness is coming to the fore." It is the author's impression, however, that in other places the contrary is true; tribal loyalties are being renewed with a consequent weakening of denominational loyalties. This may be good in that it will force denominations together, although the formation of tribal churches should be avoided at all costs.

In those areas where there have been working comity arrangements up to the present time, the migration of people to the cities and mines brings new problems. Are the denominations going to follow all their members, or are they going to transfer them to other denominations? In the Congo and Angola, a pattern has been worked out quite successfully whereby the geographical comity arrangements are maintained, with a ready transfer of membership among most denominations. In Angola the denominational names are not generally used and all Protestants are known as Evangelicals. In the Congo most Protestants belong to the ecumenically sponsored "Church of Christ in the Congo." In Mozambique and Southern Rhodesia there is a tendency to maintain linguistic and tribal group loyalties, calling for an unwarranted geographical denominational spread and undue overlapping. The cost of such supervision, with the crisscrossing back and forth to visit churches and schools, plus the duplication in denominational headquarters is certainly an unimaginative use of limited church funds. The petty denominational loyalties which are built up, often obscuring basic loyalty to Jesus Christ, may in the long run be highly detrimental to the Christian witness.

For most Europeans, there are historical reasons for the separations within Christendom—those events have less meaning for the African. It is true that in time they will take on added significance if the denominational ties strengthen, but at the present time the gulf separating the various segments of Christendom can be spanned. Even the strained relationships between Protestants and Catholics which have existed in the predominantly Roman Catholic countries of Portugal, Spain, and Italy have not been transferred to Africa with such intensity. The tensions of the widely separate branches of the church universal are less acute among Africans than among Europeans. Perhaps the church in Africa can help unite the body of Christ. Speaking for Roman Catholicism (*The Council, Reform, and Reunion*), Hans Küng states that "Within the Church today there is a longing and striving and praying for reunion of a totally new power and intensity." May the beginning made by "good Pope John" be continued by his successor!

Fundamentally, the desire to be related more closely to a world organization turns many African churchmen towards union and closer affiliation with the World Council of Churches. Africa has been isolated for so long that there is an intense desire to know what is going on in the rest of the world. Ties with London, Stockholm, Oslo, Paris, or New York are gratifying, in part, if no more universal ties can be made. But it is to Geneva and the World Council that many African churchmen look with longing eyes, just as African statesmen look to the United Nations. There is something about a world outlook which appeals to

Africans and should appeal to all Christians. Perhaps it is part of the new self-consciousness which wishes to find outlets beyond the confines of the African continent; perhaps it is a desire to join some world body for the travel benefits that might be derived; perhaps it is God's Spirit moving over the face of Africa and the world. Whatever it may be, African churchmen have this intense desire to reach out far and wide for association and fellowship with those of a like mind from other parts of the world, and at times this may mean bypassing denominational ties and loyalties.

A child is rightfully sheltered from evil influences when he is young and innocent. As he grows to adolescence and maturity, he can no longer be shielded from all undesirable influences. Africans are *not* children. If they ever needed protection, most of the mature churchmen have reached the stage where they will and *must* decide for themselves what influences are harmful and what beneficial. The developing church in Africa probably will first strengthen its ties with like-minded denominations within the national boundaries, and then reach out for fellowship on a world basis, even though the denomination founding that fellowship may look askance at the World Council of Churches because of its reputedly liberal tendencies.

Although in Angola, Mozambique, and Southern Rhodesia, African churchmen are not yet in top leadership positions of the existing National Christian Councils or their counterparts, many are exerting very real pressure to break the denominational ties in favor of closer association with other groups within the national area and with a world organization. A fairly representative and influential group of African churchmen in Southern Rhodesia are quite vocal in the denunciation of the existing interdenominational organ—the Southern Rhodesia Christian Conference. Its nonrepresentative nature does not permit it to participate in current social issues and there is a reluctance to join the World Council of Churches. Unless European denominational heads move more rapidly toward closer ties within the national boundaries, as well as with the World Council of Churches or the World Evangelical Fellowship, the trend toward rebellion and fragmentation may increase. This does not necessarily mean to move away from the church universal, but rather from European domination.

On the other hand, one cannot be too optimistic about the future solidarity of the church under African leadership if the present tendency toward redivision under African-led denominations and sects is any forecast. The fragmentation of the church —the body of Christ—is more pronounced under predominantly Protestant-influenced and European-dominated areas.

None of the foregoing should discourage church leaders in Africa—cooperation and unity do not just happen! Patient and unceasing effort is required; the cause is worth the toil and the goal demands it. Jesus said, ". . . there shall be one fold and one shepherd" (JOHN 10:16, KJV).

Part II

THE CHURCH AND ITS WITNESS

A TRIBUTE TO MISSIONARIES

Not long ago, a well-known African journalist, Pius Wakatama, wrote in the *Daily News*: "Some politically conscious Africans say that missionaries are the worst thing that ever happened to Africa. . . . All straight-thinking people, of course, know that this is not true. Missionaries are, in fact, Africa's greatest benefactors. . . . Missionaries are not following the dictates of earthly masters. They are carrying out the orders of Jesus Christ."

As a young missionary in Angola I often pushed aside the tall grass to read the inscription on an isolated tombstone marking the place some pioneer missionary was buried. Just before he died, Melville Cox said, "Though a thousand fall, let not Africa be given up." And it has *not* been given up!

The early history of the William Taylor Self-Supporting Mission in Angola notes that after eleven years of missionary activity, the missionaries who had died in the call of duty exceeded the African converts! Those were the days when "Onward Christian Soldiers" had real meaning, for as the pioneers fell, others replaced them so that the work of evangelism might go forward.

The physical dangers and hardships are not nearly so great for the modern missionary, but the dedication to Christ and His Kingdom is no less. Paul said, "I beseech you therefore, brethren, by the mercies of God, that ye present your bodies a living sacrifice, holy, acceptable unto God which is your reasonable service" (ROMANS 12:1, KJV). A lesser commitment will not withstand the pressures of modern Africa.

Modern missionaries must have the stamina to face death in Krugersdorp, prison sentence in Angola, criticism in Rhodesia, persecution in Mozambique, bullets in Katanga, hostility in the Sudan, indifference in Algeria. Their dedication to Christ—originally made years ago, but renewed each dawn—sustains them in the midst of hostility.

This is not to say that missionaries are approaching sainthood! An objective but positive evaluation was given by a newcomer—close to, but just outside, the official missionary force—my secretary, Robert Lee Stuart:

> I am not particularly shocked by the humanness of those directing the mission effort of the church. I was perhaps adequately enough warned about the fact that "missionaries are people" not to be disillusioned by squabbling over furniture, arguments over children's education, griping in regard to appointments, etc. What surprises me is that they give so much and live such useful lives, in spite of personal limitations and those imposed upon them by the situations in which they live. I pay tribute at the outset to those, who, year after year, are doing difficult tasks daily which I don't think I could perform for a week without collapsing. Most missionaries don't live in grass huts and cook over wood fires out in the bush; they have a reasonable number of the necessities, and even some of the luxuries which life can afford. But the "hardships of the spirit" are very real, and very difficult; far more demanding are emotional stresses and strains, spiritual anguish and social isolation than any physical limitations which may be imposed. I am deeply moved when I see people reacting to these pressures with sincere Christian love—not brooding over their own misfortunes, but reaching out in positive witness for their faith.

If they can maintain their poise and perspective, swaying with the winds of change instead of being uprooted, the missionaries can become the heroes of the church in Africa!

8

Jesus Christ

THE MAJOR CONTRIBUTION that Christianity can make anywhere in the world is the presentation of Jesus Christ, the Son of God. It is He who makes Christianity different from other religions. He becomes a uniquely vital force both in the lives of individuals and in the life of a community or a nation. It is His mind and His spirit which can transform; it is His presence which can restrain the howling wind and calm the waves of violence. He is doing that in Africa today.

Jesus Christ is more than the Son of Mary; He is God's very gift to the world. One may not be able to understand the nature of His conception in the womb of the virgin, which gave Him His divine start in life—nor could one necessarily understand the nature of His life were He only human, for surely no man before or since has lived like Him. It is more His matchless life than the account of His conception that convinces the believer that Jesus Christ is very God. It is He whom the church presents as God's gift to Africa.

The preaching of the gospel cannot be dissociated from the preacher although the message may be greater than he who proclaims it. Neither can the missionary program be dissociated from the missionary who serves as Christ's servant in Africa and around the world. Missionaries are the primary carriers of the gospel to the non-Christian world although the Christian witness has been enhanced or marred by Christians following a so-called secular profession. Missionaries have heard the commission, "Go ye," and they have volunteered. They have been sent —often not knowing where they were going—happy in the opportunity to carry out Christ's great commission. The world owes a debt of gratitude to this corps of noble people.

The Gospel narratives tell us that as an Infant, Jesus spent some time in Africa. Therefore, as He returns to Africa, He is part of her own contribution to God's world Kingdom. He is one with God; it is He whom Africa needs to make her whole.

Long before the missionaries arrived on the scene, religion was a very vital force in the lives of African individuals and of the groups known as tribes. Each tribe had its own theory of creation, and some of these stories did not differ greatly from the Jewish account found in Genesis.

One of these traditional tales recounts that in the beginning, the Old One who was there already—the Great One—felt in a creative mood. He took reeds of the marsh and carved figures from them, then he gave them life and turned them loose to wander over the hills and down into the green valleys where there was fresh water. They found their way to the prairies and thence down the rivers to the great expanses of water.

Although different in form, they all had one thing in common; they were dissatisfied. The elephant, proud of his strength, wished to have the added fleetness of the antelope, which in turn coveted the power of the elephant. The eagle wanted some of the speed of the swallow. The cunning leopard preferred the zebra's stripes to his own spotted fur. All of the animals, birds, and fish were complaining.

The Great One, the Old One, became so bothered by all these requests for change that he ordered the spider to build him a ladder high up into heaven. When it was completed, the Old One climbed to the top, cutting the ladder so that it fell back to earth. He continues up there far away, but the objects of his creation are here below. Communication between here and there is very difficult; but the creator still exists. He makes his presence known through the thunder, earthquake, and lightning. His continued interest in the objects of his creation is evidenced through the warmth of the sun and the refreshing rain. At times he appears to selected people in certain places but, for the masses, his presence is slightly felt—occasionally he may show his pleasure or his anger in the events of life.

In this context, one can see the significance of the story of Jesus Christ, brought to Africa by the missionaries: God had not isolated Himself permanently, but was moved with compassion by the wandering and suffering of His people; and He sent His Son into the world to teach the more perfect way of life. To this Person and to His way of life the African people have turned in unprecedented numbers.

During His earthly ministry, there was the desire to see Him, to touch the hem of His garment, to feel the nail prints in His hands. So today the people of Africa would see Jesus. But, more important, they need to know the quality of His life. They need to know Him, and through Him to better understand the Great One who was from the beginning. They, like all people, need to feel the warmth of His personality—need to experience the transforming power of His love. He is God's gift to man everywhere. He is the connecting link between the past and the present; He is the bridge between humanity and divinity. By His suffering and death, He became the Mediator between man and his Creator. It is Christ who alters personality and so reorients an individual to himself, his community, and his God that life takes on new meaning.

The church unashamedly presents Jesus Christ as Leader of the people of Africa. People everywhere need a leader; perhaps less sophisticated people need one more keenly. The names of Churchill, DeGaulle, or Nehru indicate that this is not a peculiar need of any racial or national group. Traditionally there has been a ready acceptance of strong leadership in Africa; subsequent history may well revere the good qualities of Lobengula of Southern Rhodesia, Chaka of the Zulus, Queen Jinga of Angola, Gungunyana of Mozambique, and many others. The African people appreciate strong leadership, but it must be fair and just.

The qualities which Christ possesses make Him the ideal Leader. People of His day readily recognized His qualities of leadership; He attracted people; He must have had a compelling personality.

His purpose and goal were clear. He had a depth of conviction as to the significance of His mission. He was divinely inspired and divinely led. There was a special quality about Him that made people intuitively recognize that He had recourse to the Father. He was a respected Teacher. He was tender, loving, and compassionate in His dealings—sensitive to the needs of others. He enjoyed a good time socially. He was pacific in general and always nonviolent. He was progressive in that He was willing to deviate from the past. He was what today would be known as a farsighted administrator because He trained His disciples to take over after He was gone. He delegated authority and power to others. He was fair and just in all His dealings. He was willing to sacrifice and even die for the cause He represented. What a list of leadership qualities! He still has them today. The church presents Christ as Leader, to all who need guidance.

The sense of fellowship has been very strongly developed among the African people. One might even go so far as to say that the African ideal was to live in a village where no one tried to harm another and each joined in mutual helpfulness. In such an association one could find a sense of community—each was esteemed and desired by others of the group; apart from his group, life had little meaning. There was a great desire to be in harmony with one's friends and associates as well as with the spirits of his ancestors.

This typical African idea of community is not too different from the New Testament concept of the Kingdom of God, except in its exclusion of nonmembers of the group. All that is needed is the strong personality of Jesus Christ and the power of God to make such a concept of inclusive fellowship a reality. African people have a feeling for it, a longing to see it realized.

With Christ as Leader, circles of fellowship become general and inclusive—not particular and exclusive. The sign "RIGHT OF ADMISSION RESERVED" is removed and in its place one can read, "WHOSOEVER WILL MAY COME." What a difference! That is precisely what happens when Christ becomes the Head of the community.

The church presents Jesus Christ as the Saviour of all people everywhere. Africans need salvation as much as any other people for everywhere "the wages of sin is death" (ROMANS 6:23, KJV).

Salvation is wider and broader than liberation from certain proscribed sins. Salvation is freedom from sin—freedom to rise above self-imposed or inherited limitations; freedom from destructive social customs; freedom to commune with God; freedom to find a place of fellowship with others who make up the Christian community; freedom to inherit eternal life.

The church recognizes that there are certain barriers which keep man from enjoying his full freedom as a son of God. Sin always limits and enslaves man, and he will never achieve his highest stature as long as he is limited by sin. Sin is destructive; sin is negative; sin leaves scars. Sin divides and wherever there is division, there can never be the highest creativity. Sin may be considered all of those things which separate man from fellowship with God and from communion with his fellow men. The church proclaims that in Jesus Christ there is freedom from sin, for Christ came into the world to liberate man.

Everyone should have an opportunity to develop his God-given talents so that he can become a resourceful and productive member of modern society. The Christian believes that God has placed a spark of divinity and creativity within the soul of every individual and that that spark constantly urges man onward. If man is truly free and in fellowship with Jesus Christ, he will follow the upward path until more and more he becomes the image, in all of his actions, of the God who created him.

It is interesting that African youth do not react negatively to Jesus Christ. Never have I heard Him or His teaching criticized. It is readily admitted that "He is the way, the truth, the life." If only He can be liberated from His western garb! If only He can be freed from His western characteristics of the centuries! Had He come directly from Palestine to Africa, He would be more acceptable! Had He come directly up the Nile from His sojourn in Egypt, He might have won all of Africa! But, He comes from God and therefore His image is that of God Himself and His purpose is redemptive. As Simon Peter confessed, He has the words of eternal life (JOHN 6:68, RSV).

The supreme gift of the church to Africa is Jesus Christ, Son of God, Leader and Saviour of all mankind, and the exclusive possession of no one race or nation.

9

A Message

A SECOND SIGNIFICANT contribution of the Christian church is the gift of the Bible. Very few of the people have the complete Bible in their own languages, but portions of the Scriptures have already been translated into 401 African dialects—about one-half of the total number. The Roman Catholic Church (which traditionally has been somewhat reluctant to let the laity read the Bible without clerical interpretation) is reconsidering her century-old policy. When more translations are available, the spiritual awakening which always follows the circulation and reading of the Bible will come.

In the Bible we have not only the story of Jesus' life and teaching, but the long historical account of God's progressive revelation. God has always taken the initiative in revealing Himself to man. The Bible contains the story of that revelation together with an account of man's reactions to it. The experiences recorded in the Bible are those of men everywhere and through all times. The moral values given and the spiritual insights announced might at times be obscured by archaic language or symbolism, but they are nonetheless valid.

The people of Africa have legends of their forefathers' association with God. These should be conserved, compared, and contrasted with Old Testament accounts; they are of particular interest to Africa. However, there is a universality and completeness to the Bible which is needed everywhere. A young man studying in Brazil wrote, "I find that the major blessing which the white man has brought to Africa is the gospel." If the church has done no more than give the Bible to Africa, its mission will have been justified.

The Bible is a Book of many messages. These messages—to different individuals or groups—are all expressions of its one main theme that God is Love.

To those who are harassed, there is an assurance of hope. Probably no story is better loved throughout "colonial" Africa than that of Moses leading the children of Israel out of Egyptian bondage. It is political dynamite, too; for, although "Israel" and "Egypt" are the terms used, substitution of names is subconsciously made—to give the story more emotional impact.

The struggle of the children of Israel to obtain their freedom brings a quick and sympathetic response from the people of Africa today. Sometimes there is real concern over the length of time it took to get the children of Israel settled in their own country. But the fact that God was leading the Israelites, even during the forty years in the wilderness, gives Africans hope that He may be leading them, too.

The Bible message gives dignity to the dejected, despised, and downhearted; in fact, it gives dignity to *all* people because it teaches that every individual, regardless of background, is of special value in the sight of God. The section of the community from which he comes, the cost of the house in which he lives, the school which he attended, his racial characteristics or social class, his yearly income or the kind of car he drives—none of these things enter into God's evaluation of a man. God looks into a man's heart and not at the exterior drapings which surround him.

A man's stature is determined by the motivations which drive him, by the ideals which sustain him, by the determination with which he overcomes barriers, by the perseverance with which he struggles to achieve a worthy goal, and by the way he treats his fellow men in his struggle for attainment. All of these things, rather than the circumstances of his birth, are the measure of a man.

Although throughout the Bible there is significance attached to the individual, it is in the New Testament that this concept of the dignity and value of man is most clearly asserted. To Jesus it made little difference whether He was dealing with a Samaritan woman, a pillar of the synagogue, a blind beggar, an adulteress, a prince, or a little child. He had time for, and was concerned about, the welfare of all people. For those who have been traditionally rejected, this aspect of the gospel has special significance.

Several months ago a mission administrator was traveling down the east coast of Africa by plane. At Nairobi a European colonial administrator boarded the plane and struck up a conversation; the official proceeded to tell what was wrong with missions—his main complaint was that the "mission boys" have a feeling they are equal to Europeans. This is a common complaint and should be considered a compliment!

Association with Jesus Christ gives true dignity and sincere humility. At times the understanding of teen-age youth is not quite complete and they may acquire a false sense of their own importance before they are clothed with dignity and Christian humility. One of the great joys of any missionary parent is to see this first stage pass in his own children as well as in African youth (what parent doesn't!), and a true sense of the worth of human personality—including both dignity and humility—develop. It is part of the Christian heritage.

Because results of actions are so often delayed, some people find it difficult to believe that in life the reaping follows the sowing and the harvest is determined largely by the quality and quantity of the seed sowed (GALATIANS 6:7, KJV). In general, the African people have been patient in waiting for the Europeans to share the responsibilities and advantages of community life on a basis of equality; many of the former feel that the harvest time is being overly delayed; some of the latter fear that it is coming too soon. Partnership has been the avowed policy in the Federation of the Rhodesias and Nyasaland; but Lord Malvern, a former prime minister, made the unfortunate mistake of likening the partnership to that which exists between a rider and his horse! The comparison has not been appreciated by the Africans—they are tired of being the horse and think it is time to climb into the saddle! In similar vein, the Portuguese have long been proud of their policy of assimilation, which at one time might have worked. However, it has long since been doomed to failure because of the "tongue-in-cheek" way in which it was applied to Africa. After over four hundred years of Portuguese domination, less than five percent of the African population has been assimilated into the Portuguese cultural stream.

Is it any wonder that after four hundred years, the people in Mozambique and Angola are tired of patiently waiting for the harvest of their obedient labors?—or that the Rhodesian Africans think it is time for the rider to get a different horse?

The seed *will* determine the nature of the crop—the fields are now white unto the harvest. Yes, the harvest time will come soon, even in South Africa.

The Bible gives adequate warning to the violent revolutionist that "all they that take the sword shall perish with the sword" (MATTHEW 26:52, KJV). The New Testament cautions restraint even though in the Old Testament bloodshed was often justified. One should not forget the Holy Wars—the Crusades—which will always be a humiliating blotch on the pages of church history.

The Christian does not resist evil with more evil, but resorts to those practices which may produce change without harming those who oppose him. He recognizes the difference between oppression and the oppressor. He refrains not only from violence of action but violence of spirit and attitude as well. Confronted with a situation in His own life which meant either death or the use of force to destroy others, Jesus chose to suffer personally— He did not resist force with a greater force for destructive purposes.

To the bereaved, the gospel always brings a message of comfort. To the African, the hope of immortality comes as a confirmation of what he has always believed, what his forefathers for centuries have believed. Immortality is no question mark for the average African; the resurrection is a phenomenon in keeping with his own traditions. Thus, the gospel comes as a confirmation of a belief long held.

Over and over again, the author has had the privilege of attending African funerals. Certain practices have impressed me: the making of a shelf in the side of the grave so that the dirt is not thrown directly on the casket; a hollow reed extending from the corpse to the surface of the earth to permit easy passage for the spirit of the deceased to return to its former abode; offerings of food and drink placed on the grave to satisfy the desires of the spirit, should it return. The Biblical confirmation of the belief in immortality is appreciated by Africans.

At times the Bible comes with a message of encouragement or hope; at times it gives a warning or reprimand; again it counsels restraint or makes an affirmation. But it comes with a message from God to man to be heard and heeded by all.

10

Revolution

THE CHURCH IN any part of the world should feel alarmed when no change is taking place. Such a static condition is a sure sign that its adherents are not practicing Christianity. Christianity is real; it touches all of life. If the followers of Christ are true to Him, they will be deeply conscious of their own faults; they will also see people all around them who need helping and transforming, and they will act.

Jesus' strongest opposition came from people who feared change and who got the impression that He was trying to change things. It was not those whom Jesus changed who held Him under suspicion; it was those in top positions in synagogue, society, and government; they had too much to lose. John Steinbeck wrote, in *Travels with Charley*, "It is the nature of a man as he grows older . . . to protest against change, particularly change for the better. . . . The sad ones are those who waste their energy in trying to hold it back, for they can only feel bitterness in loss and no joy in gain."

Those mature, important people of Jesus' day undoubtedly looked with pity on the beggars, the outcasts, the blind and halt whom Jesus helped; but their very pity revealed the fact that they felt themselves superior beings. They could not comprehend Christ's spirit when they had that superior feeling; only a feeling of brotherhood with all of mankind could make it possible for them to understand Him.

People who live comfortably in any land do not, as a rule, agitate for change; the children of the "haves" are not usually the rebellious youth. Unless the established people find the mind of Christ, normally they do not see any need for changes. But there are men and women and youth in Africa and other parts of the world who, in desperation, think *any* change from their present conditions would be welcome. Here lies the cause of the communist threat. It is despair at the slow and ineffective methods used by those in power which makes people turn to violence. Revolution does not have to be violent—the revolution which the church starts is nonviolent, yet it is no less a revolution.

Revolution means a drastic change in ideas or institutions; it means the transformation of people and their social patterns. It is inevitable that Christ's teachings should cause constant change for, as individuals accept the gospel, their lives are transformed. It is just as inevitable that when there are enough people with the mind of Christ, the whole pattern of society undergoes change.

As yet there is no completely Christian society. Some governments, aware that the proclamation of the whole gospel will inevitably bring about change, take steps to curtail its proclamation. In Angola and Mozambique the Portuguese authorities are very much concerned about Protestant missionaries. Therefore, they do all they can, within existing international treaties, to curtail the Protestant witness. This is in keeping with policies still practiced in Portugal, Spain, and Italy, as well as in some South American countries. In spite of the late Pope John's heroic effort to unite Christendom, his spirit of tolerance, unity, and freedom has not yet permeated throughout the Roman Catholic Church.

The gospel is inescapably revolutionary. Take, for instance, the single passage: ". . . thou shalt love thy neighbour as thyself" (LEVITICUS 19:18). Were this single concept followed conscientiously, the world would be changed overnight. There is no more potent force in the world than the love of Christ in the hearts of men.

Being a Christian is no simple matter. All of us are so concerned with ourselves that it is difficult indeed to be equally concerned for all other people. The demands of the gospel are frightening. Many people who know well the story of the Good Samaritan and theoretically accept Jesus' answer to the question,

"Who is my neighbor?" fall far short of following His teaching. In a divided society such as that in southern Africa and the southern United States the problem arises in determining which neighbor.

Several years ago, I spoke to the residents of the African Girls' Hostel in Umtali, Southern Rhodesia, about the impelling force of love. The African matron was interpreting. In the course of the talk, the question arose, "And *who* is my neighbor?" It was a rhetorical question at first. Then, thinking it should be more than that, I turned to the matron and asked, "Mai, are you my neighbor?" She was hesitant at first; then, as the application of the story dawned, she answered, "According to the gospel, yes." There it is! According to the gospel, love knows no barriers of class or race or nationality. According to the gospel, old patterns of life must give way to new. Love will not permit a "horse and rider" concept of relationships to prevail between different segments of society.

Even the force of nuclear weapons is not so potent as the gospel when it comes to changing lives and altering social patterns. In *African Nationalism*, the Reverend Ndabaningi Sithole tells of a conversation between two Africans. The first was complaining about the alienation of the land to Europeans. The second replied, "When Europeans took our country, we fought them with spears, but they defeated us because they had better weapons. And so colonial power was set up, much against our wishes. But lo! the missionary came in time and laid explosives under colonialism. The Bible is now doing what we could not do with our spears."

Rarely if ever have Protestant leaders of the church been directly involved in the overthrow of any government; but there is something dynamic about the gospel which works as a leaven in all society for the betterment of mankind. During the past five years, more than a hundred million people in Africa have found their political freedom in probably one of the least bloody transfers of power in history. Father Trevor Huddleston, Anglican priest from Sophiatown, expelled from the Republic of South Africa, and now Bishop of Masasi, in Tanganyika, was quoted in *The Rhodesia Herald:* "The overwhelming fact about Africa in its day of freedom is not its violence, but its lack of violence."

The church starts a revolution with its program. One of the primary tenets of the church program is to meet the felt needs of people. Think for a moment about the single item of education. The Reverend T. A. Beetham, in his paper, "The Changing Front of Christian Education in English-Speaking Africa," given to the All Africa Churches Conference on "Education in a Changing Africa" in January of 1963, contrasted the program of the African pastor-teacher of thirty years ago with today's more modern program. Sketchy as the education of thirty years ago was, it produced great change. The pastor-teacher taught much more than the little knowledge he had mustered out of books.

"He had no idea how revolutionary a person he was. Every day that those boys devoted to his scanty curriculum was a day not spent in following their uncles to the farm or forest or chief's court; a new education was taking the place of the old. . . . He was introducing new, and usually mixed, patterns of what was the 'good' life. . . ."

God has divided His gifts fairly evenly among His various children of all races. In some activities one may excel; a different individual may be superior in others. But it would seem that for any lack in one area of life, God has abundantly compensated with other gifts so that in the end there is no overall superiority or inferiority. Achievement and failure are both known to all.

Often a lack of achievement is attributable to limited training. Whether colonial governments have deliberately followed a policy of restricted training for Africans is difficult to say; it is irrefutable that subtropical southern Africa has been limited in the amount of education available for Africans. Often those who have gone overseas for degrees have been encouraged, if not sponsored, by churches or by individual missionaries. As these students have pursued advanced studies, either overseas or in their own countries, they have reached a growing consciousness of their personal rights and their duty to achieve self-determination for their people. With few exceptions, the leaders in the independence movements in the various countries of Africa have been educated, at least partially, in Christian missions. Is it largely because of this that the drive toward independence has been so nonviolent? The church has provided the channel—in education—through which countless individuals have become conscious of their own place in society and now desire to raise the standards of their own people. It is true in Africa as well as in Asia that "many of those who subsequently took a leading part in the national struggle acquired their dominant ideas through their university education" (*Revolution and Reconstruction, S.C.M. of India*).

Again, in her administrative practices, the church has fostered major changes in standards of living and outlook upon life. When an African educator came back from his three years in London with a master's degree in education, it was only natural that he should be placed in a position of administrative responsibility commensurate to his long years of teaching experience and his advanced training. He was accordingly appointed headmaster of a new and higher teacher-training college. When the Southern Rhodesian newspapers heard of the appointment, it became a news item. Here was an inviolable tradition broken: it was not customary in Southern Rhodesia to appoint an African headmaster above the primary level! This was moving too fast! And think of it—he was to have European teachers under his direction! What a scandal! It wouldn't work! But it did.

Now, at that same Old Umtali Centre, with nearly a thousand pupils and over thirty teachers (about a third of them Europeans), there is an African chairman of station, an African principal of schools, an African headmaster of the secondary school, and an African headmaster of the primary school. The church constantly breaks traditions and social mores which, according to the gospel, are untenable. By so doing, she makes it clear that her mission is to conform not to existing patterns, but rather to the concepts of her risen Lord.

The church is responsible for change by her very presence. For many years, when a district missionary made his visitations, he knew that his presence as a representative of the church created a stir in the community. Preparations for his visit were carefully made well in advance; all the cutlery of the village was collected, sorted, selected; the few glass tumblers were washed and polished. The choice bananas and pawpaw were carefully picked and ripened. Nests were robbed of the fresher eggs for breakfast. Perhaps a hunt would be organized the day before the expected arrival, or, failing to find wild game, a village rooster might be sacrificed. All of that hustle and bustle because a representative of the church was coming for a visit! In the process, new patterns of community cooperation were being initiated. And, if those long evenings in the African pastors' homes were as meaningful to others as they were to me, new values in human relationships were being established. Those values are still valid and even today are gnawing away at any bands of enforced segregation.

Some missionaries feel that staying with African pastors and teachers puts too much strain upon the African community. It is a needed and desired strain. It does have some complications, however, for the missionary. Having accepted the hospitality of the pastors and teachers on his district, he must, in turn, invite them to stay in his home. A reciprocity develops through the years which is most meaningful to the missionary and his family and ought to be equally meaningful to his African colleagues.

Yes, the church has brought changes to Africa, as it has in many other parts of the world; and, if given the opportunity, it will continue to do so. Ambassador Chester Bowles states, in *Africa's Challenge to America*, "The interest of many African leaders in such revolutionary ideas as individual liberty, the potential dignity and capability of all men and, through an inevitable process of logical extension, self-government, has its source in the Christian faith. Thus the Christian missionaries and their Book have been in this very practical sense Africa's true revolutionaries."

What has happened in Africa has had a direct bearing upon the struggle for civil rights in the United States. Although equality for Negroes would eventually have come in all the States, as it will come in southern Africa, the independence of African countries has greatly hastened the process. The presence in the States of so many African diplomats and students has made segregation an increasing embarrassment. The weight of world opinion provides considerable pressure in international politics and gives support for decisions of primarily internal concern. Thus the bread cast upon the waters (ECCLESIASTES 11:1), through the sending of missionaries, has returned to feed those waiting for equal rights in the United States.

11

Education

THE CHURCH HAS done so much in the field of education in Africa that some assume it alone is responsible for educating a whole continent. Dr. Eduardo C. Mondlane of Mozambique wrote, in *Old Roots in African Education*, "It can even be said without exaggeration that the Christian missions were responsible for demonstrating to the rest of the European people that Africans were also capable of engaging in the same intellectual pursuits as all other racial groups. For quite a long time Christian missions bore alone all the responsibilities of planning, financing, and running the schools in Africa, with little help from colonial governments."

In the beginning, the church took nearly all of the responsibility for formal education. Richard Gray in *The Two Nations*, writing about Southern Rhodesia as late as 1919, says, "The Government, however, still took no direct part in the main field of Native education; mission schools were given increasing grants, but they received relatively little attention from officials in the Education Department, who were primarily concerned with the work of European and Coloured schools."

Gradually the various governments in Africa have taken over more of the responsibility, especially in providing finances, until today the education of African pupils is generally recognized as a three-way cooperative project involving the churches, the governments and the parents participating in payment of fees and helping to provide buildings.

During the early years of mission schools, the response of the African people was generally negative. Gifts were often provided by missionary teachers as incentives to get children to attend school. At best, the attendance was quite irregular. About twenty years ago a noticeable change began. The advantages of education impressed itself upon the rural people suddenly as they saw the earning power of their sons rise. Then began the scramble to the schools. Accepting appreciatively the increased financial aid from government sources, the church still was not able to keep pace with the demand. Even by straining its own finances and personnel to the maximum, the church has had to turn many children away from existing institutions.

As might be expected, parents—instead of expressing appreciation for the three children they may have in school—often concentrate on the one or two who can't find a place and blame the church for its inability to provide for *all*. A second result of this rush toward the school has been the inability to give the quality education which the church would like to give. As a result, many pupils pass through the schools of the church without getting the kind of moral encouragement and instruction in character building which they should have. In spite of the rather prevalent criticism against the church for not being able to provide adequately either quantitatively or qualitatively, there is a growing appreciation on the part of mature, educated adults for the contribution which the church has made.

According to 1960 statistics (and statistics are not always reliable) only about 40 percent of all children in Africa of primary school age are enrolled in classes. In some countries, such as Southern Rhodesia, the percentage is now 95.1; in Mozambique and Angola it falls slightly below the 25 percent mark. The world average is just under 50 percent.

It is at the secondary or high-school level that the gap is most felt at the present time; only 3 percent of African youth of that age group is in school, as compared to a 31 percent world average. At the university level, only 1 *African youth out of* 500 is in school! In Britain 20 out of every 500 young people are entering universities; the Russian figure is 60 out of every 500; in the United States, it is still higher. In December of 1962, M. S. Adiseshiah, Assistant Director General of UNESCO, estimated that the world over, 5 percent of the young people are attending universities.

This means that although the church has made a noble start in bringing schools to Africa, it has only made a beginning. It is encouraging to note the interest of the newly-independent countries of Africa, as well as some of those still under colonial rule, in meeting this crucial demand for more adequate educational facilities. Implementing the recommendations of the Addis Ababa UNESCO conference of May 1961, some governments are committed to provide over one-fifth of their total national budget for the development of education, Donald M'Timkulu reported in December of 1962. Dr. M'Timkulu is the first general secretary of the Continuing Committee of the All Africa Churches Conference, and one of Africa's most respected leaders.

In some countries in Africa, there have been deliberate restrictions imposed against the Protestant Church in the field of education. In Southern Rhodesia over 40,000 pupils are enrolled in Methodist mission schools, but in adjacent Mozambique there are less than 1,000. Further pending restrictions may force our church to give up *all* formal educational activities there.* In view of the limited facilities provided by the government and government-sponsored Roman Catholic schools these restrictions are especially tragic.

People have asked why the church's involvement in education in Africa is so heavy. Five reasons might be given:

First is the continued *need to train Christian workers.* The early missionaries realized the need for literacy among those who would transmit the gospel. They understood that often the most effective carriers of the message were those with some formal education. Thus, both Protestant and Catholic churches attempted to train pastors and priests. This was true in the pioneer days in the United States and everywhere else in the world where the church has gone. As the educational level of the masses has risen, there has been the ever-growing demand for more adequate preparation for those engaged directly in the work of propagation of the faith. If the church is to be planted in Africa (or anywhere else), the primary responsibility for its administration and propagation must pass to the national or indigenous peoples.

* Word has recently been received that threatening restrictions have been relaxed and authorization officially granted for two primary schools (Escolas de Adaptacao).

Many missionaries have been noted for their exceptional vision. Recently I asked a mature African pastor (director of an institution near Salisbury, Southern Rhodesia), "How is it that your church has produced so many leaders in the African community?" I named prominent Africans in both Bulawayo and Salisbury and points in between—that particular church has an African membership of less than fifty thousand but it has produced nearly half of the current leaders in the African community, which numbers over three million. The pastor thought for a moment and then replied, "We had a missionary who inspired us." What a tribute! *There* was a missionary who thought of his pupils not as "these dumb boys" but as "these embryonic national leaders." They have more than fulfilled his dream for them.

For years, missionaries have dreamed dreams and have seen visions for their pupils; with a suggestion here, a word of encouragement there, mingled with a hard assignment here and a bit of the rod there, they have sent them forth to do the impossible. One Sunday evening not long ago, I sat watching some two hundred older youth file into Beit Hall at the Old Umtali Centre for a reception. Their strength, their vitality, their capabilities, their future—what an opportunity for some missionaries!

Second, the church has become involved because it has felt the *need to help its adherents and others come into their maximum potential as children of God*. As Senator H. Ravelomanana of Madagascar expressed it at the Conference on Christian Education in a Changing Africa, held in Salisbury in January, 1963, "If colonial administrators built schools so as to have an educated labour force, the Protestant missions on the other hand insisted on training MEN." Most of the missionaries coming to Africa were educated people. They saw the advantages of education. They might have been wiser to have tried to understand the traditional African systems of training and added to them, instead of starting anew on the western pattern of the three R's, but it is to their credit that they started something in their attempt to enrich the life of the people. Dr. M'Timkulu asserted at a 1962 Salisbury Conference, "Anyone who has read the early missionary records and letters cannot but be struck by the fact that they sought not only to free men from the bondage of sin, but also to free them from the bondage of ignorance and superstition which kept them from reaching the stature of full manhood."

Third, the church must respond to *the felt needs of the people.* Those churches which did not become involved in education in earlier years are now in the embarrassing position of trying to explain why their denomination has not been interested in intellectual development as well as in spiritual welfare. In some instances, they are now trying to atone for this lack by starting educational work; others sit by feebly and watch the most ambitious of their youth find their way to existing schools, identifying themselves with other denominations in the process. At the present time, acceptance of a denomination by African people is largely conditional upon becoming involved in education, as noninvolvement is interpreted as a lack of interest in the basic needs of the people.

Undoubtedly the church has become over-involved in education; many churchmen wish that the state would take over education as one of its responsibilities—on the condition that existing facilities be expanded (not curtailed) until education becomes universal. Although governments may be sympathetic and visualize education as a direct responsibility of government (or local communities), many are not prepared at this stage to make the drastic adjustment needed. In *The Background of Educational Development in the Federation*, Basil Fletcher states that in 1963, out of a total of 2952 primary schools in Southern Rhodesia, 2885 were administered by the churches. The government authorities realize that they do not have the personnel needed for a full educational program; they want the churches to continue to contribute the limited resources which they have traditionally provided; and, some of them recognize there is a quality in church schools which is badly needed.* The Ministries of African Education are among the most sympathetic officials toward the total program of the church in Africa. Is it because they are intimately aware of the positive impact which the church is making?

A *fourth* reason for the involvement of the church in education is *the hope of making schools tools of evangelism.* There is con-

* Since this was written, the Ministry of Education in Southern Rhodesia has announced a plan to turn lower primary education over to local communities. Details of this plan are not yet known.

siderable discussion, even within the church, as to how effective the schools have been as a means of evangelism. Some, in fact, doubt that they should even be considered as such. I am certainly aware that the schools of my own denomination have not produced great numbers of full members of the church. Partial studies reveal that the schools basically are not effective as an agency in conversion. Consequently, those missionaries who feel that the sole purpose of the church is to evangelize are keenly disappointed with the heavy involvement in schools. Others feel that the service arms of the church should be used to help people in their physical, mental, spiritual, and social needs without attempting to make converts. This group feels that services rendered in the name and spirit of Christ carry their own witness. They maintain that there should always be an opportunity for a convinced student to become Christ's disciple although coercion or intimidation should never be used to obtain such a decision.

Missionaries react differently to the demanding involvement in educational work. There are those who would withdraw immediately, whatever the consequence. They feel that the evangelistic arm of the program is penalized by the heavy responsibility in education. The more mature missionaries see education in its proper perspective and are willing to continue as long as there is a need.

Fifth, almost without exception, *the African personnel in church administration favor a continuing participation* in the educational program, with as much expansion in the higher fields as personnel and finances will allow. This probably is as important an evaluation as one can get. The African who has gone through the church schools, who loves his church and wishes it to be as effective in its witness as possible, and who at the same time is interested in the development of his people, votes in favor of continued involvement.

Dr. M'Timkulu said in a paper presented in Salisbury at the discussion on Christian Education in a Changing Africa:

> The Christian . . . is vitally concerned with education. The call to Christian mission is not only summarized in the famous imperative "go ye and preach the Gospel" but is also eternally dramatized in the parable of the Good Samaritan once we come

to realize that the battered traveler by the wayside represents not only those who have fallen among thieves in the physical sense, but also those who have been robbed of their heritage by the thieves of ignorance, superstition, lack of education and lack of opportunities.

The spread of education is thus not merely a sideline for the Christian church, but stands at the very core and centre of the Christian message bidding us in obedience to Him to see that the young are truly nurtured in His way through the family and all the other institutions that society has created for their nurture.

12

Abundant Living

MANY PEOPLE THINK that a missionary preaches the gospel and nothing else. That may be true if one gives a broad enough connotation to the word "preach." Jesus announced that He had come that His followers might have life and have it more abundantly (JOHN 10:10). It is difficult to know what comprises the abundant life for all—people differ from place to place and from time to time. Still, the church encourages all to seek a full and abundant life on earth, as well as life eternal. This does not mean that the church puts more emphasis upon the physical than upon the spiritual; the church realizes man is body and mind as well as spirit. The church tries to maintain a balance of interest between the present and the future.

Jesus said, "Ye must be born again" (JOHN 3:7); but He also said, "Give ye them to eat" (LUKE 9:13). He said, ". . . seek ye first the kingdom of God" (MATTHEW 6:33); and then He went to a wedding feast and turned the water into wine (JOHN 2:1-11). He plucked the ears of corn on the sabbath to feed His hungry disciples (MARK 2:23). In that spirit the church helps man meet *both* his temporal and eternal needs.

Although what makes up an abundant life may not be the same everywhere, six common components of the abundant life in Africa might be: a satisfactory state of health, a world perspective, a sense of belonging, economic security, an anchorage for the spirit, and a contented frame of mind. Certainly some people live an abundant life without all of these things, but these are the factors from which life takes on its deepest meaning. Jesus grew in wisdom and stature and in favor with God and man (LUKE 2:52)—a pattern which should be normal for the development of all.

The story of the high infant mortality rate and the low life expectancy in Africa a hundred years ago is too well known to repeat. To a certain extent, government medical services have followed the pattern of education: the church has pioneered with its services among the African people and increasingly the governments are moving into this field of endeavor. Either through subsidies to church institutions or through building their own establishments, governments are encouraging the well-being of the people. In some urban areas of Southern Rhodesia (such as Salisbury and Bulawayo), the hospital facilities for Africans are now superior to those for Europeans. Theoretically the Portuguese do not practice discrimination; in general, no separate facilities are made for Africans. But in the rural areas there is a dependence upon church medical institutions.

Three aspects of the medical program should be mentioned: the curative, the public health services, and the training program.

Most church hospitals are crowded to capacity. It is not unusual to find one patient in bed and a second on the floor under him. The considerate care given by doctors and nurses alike strongly recommends church-related institutions to Africans and (where it is permitted) to Europeans as well. Sr. Jose Julio Goncalves writes in his critical study of Protestant missions in Portuguese Africa (*Protestantismo em Africa*), "The Protestants, as soon as they were established, without delay gave attention to this instrument of attraction and have now an important chain of hospitals and dispensaries throughout Angola and Mozambique. . . . Such institutions constantly look after the health of blacks, whites and coloreds. Their doctors are . . . most famous. Who does not know about Dr. Parsons, Dr. Brechet or Dr. Strangway?! To these notable surgeons—and to others less well known but who equally capture the confidence of the people— many blacks, whites, coloreds, and others owe their lives. People who need medical attention see in these men high examples of brotherhood. . . . The success of Protestantism is due . . . in large part . . . to its efficient medical organization. . . ." *

The church has sent choice young people as first-class physicians, surgeons, nurses, laboratory technicians, and pharmacists to give expert diagnosis and treatment in remote and isolated parts of the world. Their dedication is especially noteworthy because of the financial sacrifice they make in order to serve as missionaries. They, especially surgeons, usually receive about a tenth of the salary they could make in the home countries. Their service has had no limit but has extended even to some of the most unfortunate of all people, the lepers. The number of leper camps established throughout Africa is a vivid testimony to the witness of the church in following the example of the Master, who went about healing the sick.

Then there are those angels of mercy who travel thousands of miles each year over rough reserve roads or open prairie to carry on the church-related public health program. The drop in infant mortality, the control of epidemics, the counseling in child care, the construction of sanitary facilities, and advice concerning nutrition are all part of the normal day's activities. These public health workers often spot serious cases and get them to established hospitals where their needs can be met.

The medical staff carries on a training program for nurses and orderlies not only for the staffing of central institutions but also for that of the ever-increasing number of dispensaries which carry on their program in even more isolated areas. Few hospitals have achieved the fame of the McCord Hospital in Durban, or the Elim Hospital in the northern Transvaal; but, though less well known, many serve quietly and efficiently in the tradition of Him who spent so much of His time curing people. A usually

* ". . . os Protestantes, mal se estabeleceram, deram, sem detenca, maior incremento a tal instrumento de atraccao, a ponto de terem chegado a possuir a mais importante rede hospitalar e assistencial em Angola e Mocambique. . . . Tais instituicoes velam permanentemente pela saude de pretos, brancos e mesticos. Os seus medicos sao, como dissemos, famosissimos. Quem nao conhece um Dr. Parsons, um Dr. Beuchat ou um Dr. Strangway?! A estes notaveis cirugioes—e outros menos conhecidos, mas que igualmente captaram a confianca das populacoes—devem a vida muitos pretos, brancos, mesticos e outros. As pessoas necessitadas de cuidados medicos veem nesses homens um alto exemplo de fraternidade humana. . . . o sucesso do protestantismo deve-se, . . . em boa parte, . . . a eficacia da sua organizacao sanitaria. . . ."

critical African student, now in India, writes, "Hospitals have cared for the people's health and have also trained nurses and medical assistants. It would be ignoring the truth if we did not appreciate this work done by missions before most governments accepted their rightful responsibility."

As I sit in my home office looking out of the window, I can see in the garden the many trees: orange, grapefruit, lemon, fig, plum, pear, mango, papaya, mulberry, guava, peach, tangerine, apricot, and banana. Some do better than others in the high altitude of Salisbury. One may lament the disappearance of indigenous fruits but he should also rejoice over the importation of so much that is new and which supplements the traditional diet. I believe it was the early Portuguese Roman Catholic missionaries who imported many of the most popular plants now used as a staple diet in Africa—maize, manioc, and sweet potato. Agricultural missionaries have improved the diet of the masses through the importation of new foods as well as through instruction in better methods of farming. The mere mention of such names as Rea, Roberts, Alvord, Schaad, Smalley and Knight has deep meaning to the people of the regions where they have labored.

Driving along a road in Mozambique, it is not unusual to hear someone exclaim, "A former Cambine student must live there!" Upon inquiry, one learns that this is evident because of the crops planted and the farming techniques used. I shall never forget a trip I took into the hinterland west of Inhambane, Mozambique. The road was very difficult because of deep sand. After traveling for some time through dreary stretches, we came upon what appeared to be an oasis. It was. There was a small settlement of better-than-average homes, each surrounded by a hedge. Beyond the houses were rows of citrus trees in full crop. Improved breeds of chickens were scratching nearby. The headman in this village had been a student at Cambine and he had profited in many ways from his time there. He was making a witness through the quiet means of farming—all was done in the name of Christ.

The second prerequisite to abundant living may be questioned by many. Is a world perspective a valuable part of life? Most of the underdeveloped countries have been quite inaccessible to outside contacts. Progress has come largely at those points where cross-fertilization of ideas has been possible and constant. Even within a given country, the more backward areas are usually those where isolation is greatest. The wider, the more varied, and the more constant the contacts, the more rapidly the process of acculturation goes on.

I have much sympathy for those who question whether Africa is gaining or losing from her outside contacts. "Uncontaminated" Africa certainly did have her charm *but* she cannot remain isolated from the rest of the world and still enjoy the advantages of world civilization. If one accepts as inevitable and desirable a growing world culture to which every country will contribute, then one will find that the church has given much to Africa.

"The church has made a breakthrough," claims one African student, "in fostering among the African people a more modern way of life. This has, in a way, helped Africa to become more internationally conscious and to develop the right desire to mix and to be on a par with the rest of the world in all aspects." Sometimes the process of getting a world perspective is painful for the African. I remember vividly the reaction of an honorable member of the Nyasaland government who arrived in New York for the first time on a bleak, cold day in December of 1962. Going through the immigration and customs formalities, the ride into New York City at the height of rush-hour traffic, the bleakness of Manhattan in late afternoon, the penetration of icy blasts from the East River—all made a terrible impact upon the new arrival. He remarked to a friend, "If this is civilization, give me Africa!"

From the time of David Livingstone to the present, missionaries have penetrated ever deeper into the interior, taking with them much that is good. Increasingly, Africans have traveled far to make their contributions to world gatherings as well as to derive benefits. The church has made a widening circle of contacts possible, and the mutual exchange of viewpoints and culture has been beneficial; Africa has much to *give* to other cultures as well as much to *gain*.

One of the basic needs of man is to belong—to feel that he is wanted and needed. Western civilization has so "atomized" the world and society that the rugged individualist of the west may not feel this need so much as his African brother, who has just recently emerged from the closely knit tribal society. Yet we are told in such books as *The Organization Man* (William H. Whyte, Jr.) that the era of rugged individualism has been tried and found wanting even in the United States, and that youth is seeking security in large organizations.

In group programs at urban Christian social centers, in church group activities for men, women, and youth, and especially within the overall fellowship of the church, this sense of belonging is provided for de-tribalized Africa. Throughout the Republic of South Africa and Southern Rhodesia, it is quite common to see groups of African women, all dressed exactly alike, converging upon a given point. It may be a church in the city, a rural school, or just under a spreading tree. They are going for their weekly meeting of the Rukwadzano—their women's society. Through this weekly fellowship, they are recreated and undergirded by their common goals and by the fellowship which has been established.

Economic security has been overstressed as a positive contribution to Africa. The assumption which some colonial nations have —that all the African people want is a full stomach—is erroneous. That was the philosophy of the Belgians, and it failed to satisfy the Congolese. A similar philosophy will fail in Southern Rhodesia and in the Republic of South Africa. The appreciation of Africans for nonmaterial values is as great as—if not far greater than—those of the materialistic west. Spiritual and social values are appreciated by Africans as much as by westerners, if not more so.

However, the importance of economic security should not be underestimated. Everyone wants security in the impersonal world that exists today, and everyone *needs* it. The church has made some contributions in this field through its training program and teaching of the values of simple, Christian living.

Man is also a spiritual being and needs anchorage to the past and hope for the future. To hear the African youth of today speak, one might judge that the church has largely failed in this most important part of its task. Attendance at an annual camp meeting of the Rukwadzano in Southern Rhodesia would give quite a different impression—as the women pray, sing, and testify at the great mass meetings (sometimes numbering five thousand), there is a strong evidence of spiritual anchorage to the past and implicit faith as far as the future is concerned. One feels, rather than sees, the great cloud of witnesses of which Saint Paul speaks (HEBREWS 12:1). Although the church may unwisely have minimized the importance of the part played by ancestors, it *has* brought sensitive Africans in touch with God's great eternal Spirit, who is ready and able to guide responsible believers everywhere.

Abundant living, however, is largely a frame of mind. Paul said that he knew how to be exalted and how to be abased, how to abound and how to be denied; but, under all circumstances, he also knew how to be content (PHILIPPIANS 4:12). That is the contribution toward abundant living which the church can give to all.

Many missionaries have lived in stick-and-mud houses without benefit of running water or glass windows. They have used a bucket, perforated at the bottom, for showers, and followed a path out back. They have gone to town for groceries and mail once a month. Water has been hauled from the river. The children have been taught at home. The nearest doctor has been a hundred miles away. These have been the hardships of the pioneer life; *but* there also has been the deep satisfaction of knowing that they were within the framework of God's will—for them at that time in history. Helping to meet the need of others in an isolated community and living under rustic conditions, they have discovered the meaning of the abundant life.

13

Understanding

NO TASK IS more difficult today than trying to bridge the gap which exists between different segments of society in south central Africa. The need for bridge-building increases as the desire to have bridges built diminishes. Sometimes, deep and wide chasms which separate are much more appealing than bridges which unite. This is especially true when fear becomes a dominant motivation and concern in life.

Apartheid is basically a desire to separate people of differing backgrounds. It makes no pretense of drawing all people together into a common fellowship. Not all South Africans subscribe to apartheid, of course. In *The Christian Gospel and the Doctrine of Separate Development* the Reverend S. P. Freeland of Pretoria, South Africa, asks, "Is it possible to imagine Jesus Christ separating Himself from other people because of their race or colour or for any other reason?" He then replies, "Such an idea is preposterous and completely unbelievable. He could not, by the very nature of His being, ever have supported such a doctrine or practice as apartheid or separate development." The task of the church is to draw people together into the Kingdom of God, not to dig chasms to divide them.

Modern society in the southern part of the African continent has so many chasms that it is difficult to build bridges of understanding over all of them or to know which bridges are most important to build. Without presuming that man can ever take the initiative away from God (for He alone, through Jesus Christ, can build permanent bridges) let us consider some of the chasms which the church is trying to span in His name. There are chasms between western and traditional African cultures, between peoples of different tribes, between old and young, between political factions, and between racial groups. Someone may well call out, "Let the church first heal herself before she starts on others!" That is a reasonable suggestion, but let us assume for the time being that through building bridges for others, the church will become conscious of its own need for closer fellowship and unity. God sometimes works that way to convince people of their own needs.

Exchange of personnel is one of the best ways to arrive at an understanding of differing cultures. Although that is not the primary purpose of scholarship programs, they *do* promote cultural exchange. So far, scholarship programs have been largely one way; but the time will soon be coming—with the development of more universities in Africa—when it can be mutual. Today, the large number of African students in Europe, Asia, and the Americas will do much toward bringing about cultural understanding. The church is certainly not alone in this program, but the church is deeply involved. Current programs in Morningside College at Sioux City, Iowa, in which some twenty families or single students from Africa and Latin America are following the university course, may be a model in this field of cultural exchange and understanding. Certainly the church people of northwest Iowa (who largely support the students) are bound to know much more about Africa and the other Americas than ever before, and the student families there are going to have a better idea of midwestern United States.

I remember well the reactions of one student to life in the United States:

REMEMBER THREE IMPORTANT THINGS:
First of all, this country is wonderful, so wonderful that the world could be saved and be a better place to live in if the *best* in it was taken by individuals and other countries.

Secondly, on the other hand, it has some very evil things. If an individual or a country took only the *evil* side, it could only lead to a condition best described as *hell*.

The third is that there are some things which are not necessarily bad, but if we who do not belong here adopted such practices or customs, then we would find ourselves outcasts to our own communities or society. It is accepted here, for instance, that a son may pat his mother on the buttocks in an innocent way, and it is perfectly sinless. But will you be able to do that as an African without causing suspicion? What would the society think of you? Another example is women putting on shorts or long trousers.

That student now has his master's degree and is returning to Southern Rhodesia soon. Because of his knowledge of life in the United States, he himself will become a bridge of understanding! The same is true of students whom the church has sent to universities in Europe. Said an African minister, after spending ten months in the States on a special study program, "*Now* I can understand you missionaries!" Not only could he understand, but he could and also does convey his understanding to others. This minister's wife has now gone to Denmark to help the people of northern Europe understand Africa better. She, in turn, will come back to Southern Rhodesia as an interpreter of European culture. And so, the process of building bridges of understanding goes quietly forward. One understanding student (still abroad) writes, "The missionaries' willingness to live and work within the African society helped the Africans to adjust themselves to the new environment in which the western civilization had come."

There was a time when the church felt that it had broken down tribalism in Africa. It is beginning to realize that this is one of those bridges which has to be rebuilt. This is not to say that *nothing* has been done in this area of conflict, but the chasm is still there.

At least one church in the Congo was sadly divided when the leaders of two parties, both active members of the same fellowship, separated on matters of political policy. Said one of the men, "When I sit across the conference table from my rival, I can look deep into his eyes and see that we are still brothers. Then I look at his advisers and cannot find any understanding." It is good to know that in spite of current differences brought about by the sudden upheaval in Africa, individuals can look deeply into each others' eyes; if this is so, a basis of common understanding can be found. In the meantime, the church must continue to proclaim the demands of the gospel for supreme loyalty to Jesus Christ which relegates lesser loyalties to a secondary place. Filling the chasms of centuries with sufficient love and discernment to provide unrestricted social intercourse is no small task. In spite of occasional breakdowns, an intertribal passage is being built.

A bridge is desperately needed between the generations in Africa. The impact of western civilization has come so suddenly that many in the older generation cannot comprehend it. Perhaps nowhere else in the world—surely at no other time in history—has the age-gap been greater than in modern Africa. A little over a year ago I was speaking to about 180 high-school students at an assembly; I asked how many had parents who had attended high school. There was one hand. Thinking that the students, accustomed as they are to British English or Africanized English, may not have understood my Americanese, I repeated the question. There was no further response. The one girl stated that her father had been to high school, but had not finished. Basically, this is true throughout Africa. The high school, and even more the university, students are pioneering in education at their level. Their parents have great difficulty in helping them with intellectual and social problems, for rapid changes have made their problems peculiar to this generation of Africans.

The rapid migration to the cities has made the youngsters' temptations far different from those experienced by their parents when they were growing up in rural areas. Many of the old restraints fall away as youth goes to the city. Often new ideas and ideals have not yet built up a set of ethical controls equal to the old. As one mother complained, "My daughter and I do not understand each other. We do not have the same interests or even speak the same language. I speak to her in Shona and she replies in English." This gulf between the generations is everywhere, but perhaps in no other place is it so wide as in Africa.

The World Council of Churches' invitation to Christian youth to meet in Nairobi, Kenya, after Christmas, 1962, was an attempt to approach the problem from the youth angle. Various groups have begun to hold family life institutes, family camp programs, Christian family conferences, in addition to the observance of

Christian home and family week. A consciousness of the magnitude of the problem is just dawning, but a beginning *has* been made. Few are aware of the attempts made by Christians to bring political leaders together and to influence them so an understanding can be reached for the common good. Many of these attempts have failed but they are none the less sincere, and perhaps from the attempts some good has emanated.

Several months ago, half a dozen church leaders in Salisbury appealed to Prime Minister Sir Edgar Whitehead to open talks with the leaders of the now-banned African party, ZAPU (Zimbabwe African People's Union), in the hope of relieving some of the tensions. The Prime Minister did not agree with the churchmen as to the seriousness of the situation and consequently did not open the door for talks. Only time will tell who was right. At any rate, the church *tried* to build a bridge that might have led to fuller understanding and cooperation.

In other areas of public life, the church has tried to become a bridge even though it has been misunderstood for doing so. Probably no group has been so effective in this field of Christian endeavor as the Quakers. Their unselfishness, their spiritual approach, their lack of publicity, their sincerity of purpose, and their active outreach in trying to find a common ground of understanding have endeared them to all who see the need for building bridges. Recently an American Quaker family, living in Salisbury, had an African guest in their home for afternoon tea. When some of their neighbors learned about this, a petition was circulated requesting the landlord to expel these missionaries from their rented home. The missionaries were sensitive (and sensible) enough to agree to surrender the contract and sought lodging in a more liberal section of the city. There they continue to entertain Africans and to build bridges of understanding.

One of the tragedies of Africa is that the European, although perhaps in daily contact with the African, does not understand him. So often the colonist, because of his dealings with the unlettered farm laborer, assumes that all Africans are as passive and inarticulate as his farm help. Because their daily contacts are with the untutored, these Europeans underestimate the strength and charm of the university graduate. They also fail to realize that he may be their superior in knowledge and culture.

Several months ago, the African headmaster of one of the church's teacher-training colleges was having lunch in a missionary's home in Salisbury. As they were finishing, a European acquaintance who had only a high-school education came by on a business matter. When he was introduced to the African (who incidentally has an M.A. from London University), the European refused to shake hands. The incident was passed off without comment, but deep emotions welled up—How could they not?—in those who were trying to bridge the gap between the races.

More than a year ago, a missionary wife invited some Europeans attending a women's convention in Salisbury to have dinner at her home. She saw no need to tell them in advance that she had an African student from Angola spending a few days with her as a house guest. The European women were seated in the living room conversing amicably when the young lady entered the room and was introduced. Immediately, a damper seemed to shut off free communication and conversation; they were forced and strained for the rest of the evening—bridges are not always wanted!

Again, a lady missionary was in a store in Umtali shopping when the headmaster of the central primary school at Old Umtali came in to buy a bottle of milk. The clerk harshly ordered the African from the store, telling him to wait at the window at the back of the store if he wished to buy anything. The missionary was so upset that she refused to make her purchases in that store. As an aftermath of this incident, the store now serves Africans and Europeans at the same counter. The headmaster concerned is now doing his theological studies at Boston University. Even when forced, bridges can be creative.

Much could be said about pastors (European and African) who are holding steady, in spite of adverse reaction from the more conservative or radical members of their congregations, in trying to make the church an all-inclusive fellowship. If bridges are going to be built in sufficient numbers to avoid complete disaster, the church leaders must take the initiative in providing avenues for people to come together, and to get to know each other. As the wife of one of the African pastors—herself a world traveler—said in a public gathering, "If I could get to know each one of you, I would surely love you."

14

Principles

THE CHURCH IS often accused of going with the tide of public opinion instead of taking a stand on Christian principles. Because of its divisions, the church has difficulty in speaking with one clear voice on the social issues of our times. However, it does not lack prophetic personalities who speak and stand on principle. In Africa there are many: the Reverend Michael Scott (formerly of South Africa); Bishop R. Ambrose Reeves (formerly of Johannesburg); Bishop Trevor Huddleston (formerly of Sophiatown in South Africa); the Reverend Colin Morris of Northern Rhodesia; the Reverend Whitfield Foy and Mr. Guy Clutton-Brock (formerly of Southern Rhodesia); the Reverend Clifford Parsons (formerly of Angola); the Reverend Andrew Doig (formerly of Nyasaland); and many others. It is interesting to note how many of these churchmen were *formerly* of various places in Africa; many of them are now *persona non grata* in certain areas of the continent because they did speak out on principle!

If one were to analyze progressive social movements such as the freedom-sitters, the citizens against the color bar, social action groups, etc., he would usually find members of Christian churches and other religious groups predominating. Often they act as individuals rather than as official delegates of their religious organizations—in other words, it is usually religious motivation which causes people to resist unjust practices.

Very often leaders in social reform are controversial characters, or they become so because of their participation in reform movements. This does not detract from their strength of character or the value of their service to their fellow men. Although some may criticize them because of their impetuosity, or what may be termed a lack of tact causing resistance to the movement which they represent, they render a valuable service to the cause of social justice and true Christianity. It may take others with different personalities and more conciliatory approaches to consolidate the gains made by the more radical reformers, but their contribution is essential.

As we consider the church's stand on principle, the recent events in Angola come immediately to mind. Probably in no other place in Africa has the church taken a firmer stand. As a result, it is being severely tested by direct government opposition in that war-torn land. What has been done is now history but perhaps, for the very sake of history, another interpretation may not be amiss. The church has taken its stand on principle against abuses permitted by the current Portuguese government.

Lest other denominations suffer reprisals because of any of my statements, I wish to state emphatically that I am not speaking for ecumenical Christianity or even for a united Protestantism. Even within my own denomination, there are those who differ radically. Consequently I speak only as an individual with a churchman's heavy administrative responsibility. I do not speak lightly!

I also wish to make it clear that I am not anti-Portuguese. Until quite recently, I have always been considered very pro-Portuguese, both within Angola and in ecumenical circles. Perhaps it was the näiveté of the young in the beginning—or just a natural loyalty to my associates—in any case, I have often found myself standing up for the Portuguese when churchmen in international and interdenominational groups have been critical. I still have a great deal of appreciation for the Portuguese people who usually treated me so courteously and hospitably.

The author and his family went to Angola in 1936. Two of our four children were born there. Three of our children grew up speaking Portuguese before they did English. Two of our children received most of their primary education in Luanda schools. For years, Portuguese was more the language of our home than English. Some of my closest personal friends were Portuguese.

It was therefore with considerable concern that I became aware of the growing spirit of rebellion among the African people, when I visited Angola on a routine administrative visit in

January, 1961. Although fear of the PIDE (secret police) was still ever-present and a number of leading laymen of the Luanda church had recently been arrested, Christians whom I had known over the years spoke openly about the hopelessness of the situation under continued Portuguese rule. Some went so far as to say that it made little difference what happened to them personally; they were willing to be sacrificed in order that their children might have more freedom in the years ahead. Sensitive missionaries were aware that the situation was pointing toward an impending crisis.

The trip, throughout the conference, convinced me that something was going to explode if nothing were done to stop it. Upon my return to Luanda (the capital), I tried to see the Governor General to lay this concern before him, but as sometimes happens, I was given the brushoff. The situation was discussed with American consular officials who felt that I was too pessimistic and that the Portuguese government had the situation under control. The propaganda agency of the government was proclaiming that all was harmonious between the races and that the Africans were proud to be Portuguese. To prove it, the government agencies wrote speeches and directed Africans to deliver them on national holidays!

None of us were prepared for the news which broke in Luanda on the morning of early February when I returned to headquarters in Rhodesia. The night before, desperate Africans had stormed the Luanda prisons in a vain attempt to release political prisoners. After that, the situation deteriorated rapidly. According to Robert E. Estabrook of the *Washington Post*, as recorded in the Congressional Record of March 15, 1962:

> As a result of the Luanda incident, some 20 Africans were beaten to death in a cemetery. Subsequently the American consulate was stoned by a white mob and, apparently because of a misunderstanding, the car of the Consul . . . was thrown into the bay.

Mr. Estabrook was one of the comparatively few American journalists allowed to visit Angola or Mozambique soon after the uprising. Supposedly, therefore, he gathered much of his news from Portuguese sources. To continue his report:

On the night of last March 15 [that is, March, 1961] a wave of terrorism suddenly engulfed northwest Angola. Members of the Bakongo tribe, which extends across the border into the Congo, broke into fanatical violence.

Africans who had worked peacefully for decades alongside Portuguese plantation operators and managers became virtual fiends, attacking white Europeans, and other Africans as well, with field knives and similar crude weapons. From 1000 to 1,500 Africans and Europeans died in the massacres, many of them horribly mutilated.

At the time, these incidents were not reported by the press because there is strict censorship in all areas of the Portuguese empire, as under other dictatorial regimes. Such an ugly incident would alter the image Portugal was trying to create for herself abroad, as well as contradict the regime's propaganda agency at home.

A few weeks after the massacre in the north, mobs of angry Europeans (accompanied by police) marched up to the Protestant mission in the center of Luanda and broke most of the large plate-glass windows in the new administration building. Still accompanied by police, they went on to the church (in the process of being remodeled) and, with fanatic enthusiasm, smashed nearly all of its windows. Next day a mob went more than four miles to an African suburb where they used sledgehammers to break all sanitary facilities of the church's clinic and social center; they set fire to clinic records, and practically demolished the center and its equipment. Again, no publicity was given to this diabolic outburst, outside Angola, and within Angola it was interpreted as mass hysteria. This might be accepted by those who live in free countries, but those who have been long residents in countries under dictatorial regimes know that in such a situation the masses have been thoroughly conditioned to seek official authorization and, in these two incidents, police accompaniment.

The reader may well ask, "Why was there an attack upon a Protestant mission?" The author sees four possible motives: political, religious, social, nationalistic. The missionaries living in Luanda have been mostly Americans. Just prior to the demonstration, the United States had, for the first time in recent years, failed to support Portugal in the United Nations. The mission and the American Consulate are the two most obvious American institutions in Luanda, and apparently it was the United Nations vote which caused the attack on the American Consulate as well as on the Protestant mission.

It is generally accepted that in Portugal, Spain, Italy, and several Latin American countries, an intolerant and bigoted type of Roman Catholicism exists which is little known in other parts of the world. Protestant infiltration into what had long been considered a Roman Catholic domain has been responsible for much friction over the years. Whether religious intolerance fanned the fires of resentment is not known, but it might well have provided some incentive. A few years earlier, in planning for the future development of Luanda, the city fathers had placed a huge map on the wall of the city hall. The fact that they had permitted a large Roman Catholic cathedral to be sketched in the very center of the Protestant mission—on the site where the mob attacked the unfinished church—gives rise to suspicion.

That Protestant missions in general were trying to educate the African people probably caused the greatest resentment among the rank and file of the Portuguese colonists. I often felt this biting criticism of the work of the church when I was living in the Dembos area. The coffee planters, in particular, felt that the Protestant church was betraying them when it educated African boys and girls upon whom the planters depended for cheap labor. They said the church was alienating the subservient working class.

The Portuguese are a very nationalistic people and very proud of their glorious history. They resent people who interpret history differently or who cannot agree with their highly nationalistic sense of mission in the world. They react against the foreignness of non-Portuguese residents, and especially of Protestant missionaries who, they feel, "spoil" the Africans.

After the raid on the mission in Luanda I was alerted to the further deterioration of the situation by long-distance telephone, and made a hurried visit to Angola to investigate. When I arrived in Luanda, I began to hear stories of the atrocities committed by the European colonists. Many Protestant pastors were reported killed or in prison. Others had fled when they heard of the massacres being committed by Europeans *outside the area of actual conflict*. No one could get permission to visit any of the stricken areas, or to visit the pastors in prison. After word of the violence in the capital spread to the hinterland, mob action seemed to be the order of the day, especially against Protestants and church property. The fact that the government did not immediately investigate and prosecute for the violence in Luanda led many Portuguese settlers to think that they were free to follow their own impulses—which, to a large extent, they were.

Lest one who is emotionally involved because of past associations and personal ties be thought to overstate the picture, here are further excerpts from Mr. Estabrook's testimony:

> The Portuguese response [to the massacres of the north] once the first shock had worn off, was one of wholesale reprisal in kind. Settlers who had seen their families butchered did not ask questions and tended to wreak vengeance on every African they encountered. In the indiscriminate slaughter, perhaps 10,000 Africans were killed.
>
> Unquestionably some white settlers constituted themselves vigilantes after the terrorism, and Africans suspected of complicity were murdered in several areas.
>
> There are some quite harrowing tales of what happened to native pastors. They were arrested by the scores, spirited away from their families and imprisoned without trial—often on no more than a remote suspicion that they might be connected with the independence movement.
>
> Although Portuguese administrators would deny the observation, it probably is fair to say that there has been a latent suspicion of educated Africans. This suspicion broke into the open after the terrorism erupted last year in northwest Angola.
>
> The scrutiny did not exclusively concern Protestants. Eight Catholic priests, including a senior African monsignor, have been arrested in Angola, and the Catholic Church has been told, in effect, to support the government.

The author returned to Angola in mid-April, 1961, when this wholesale murder was at its height. Rumors were rampant, but little was reported even in the local press. Censorship was tightened to keep word from leaking to the international press. The situation was tense—everyone was afraid of the police and everyone else. Group meetings were avoided if possible. The tales of mass killings were appalling, especially because they involved people completely outside the area of actual fighting. After telling of these reprisal activities, often the relator would ask, "What is the church going to do?"

Or: *"Now* the church must take its stand!"

Or, those who stood to suffer most would quietly whisper: "Let the world know what is happening. We are prepared to take the consequences." If any wanted caution, they restrained themselves; the audible voice of the church was for action!—not retaliatory violence, but simply letting the world know what was happening.

The person reading casually about Africa may question why the church did not speak out earlier if conditions were such that an open revolt seemed to the Africans the only way to achieve reform. This is a reasonable question, and the church may stand judged for remaining quiet for so long. But there were reasons: up to this time, the church constituency in Angola had hoped that some peaceful transition might take place, giving the Africans more of a voice in the affairs of their own country. After the massacres, it became evident that the oft-proclaimed policy of "assimilation" was nothing but a screen behind which suppression of the African people would continue. Now the die was cast—the struggle was on. Let the leaders of the church speak for the dispossessed who had no voice because of rigid censorship. After what had already happened, the church people were ready to take the consequence of further reprisals for informing the world of events in Angola.

The church had at times raised a very feeble voice against the more glaring abuses of human rights and had promptly been spanked for doing so! A first-term missionary in Luanda wrote a letter, about 1951, to his mother in South Dakota, criticizing some abuses. The letter was printed in the local weekly Dakota newspaper and picked up by the Portuguese clipping service. The missionary was given twenty-four hours to pack and depart from Angola. After that, it was felt that it was better to have missionaries in Angola (even though silenced) then to have them all expelled. To cite another case—in 1953 an American bishop made a speech in New Bedford, Massachusetts; he reportedly made an unfavorable comparison of conditions in Mozambique with other parts of Africa. Although no publicity had been given to it, the bishop was placed on the *persona non grata* list and denied entrance into Mozambique and Angola for nearly two years, although favorable reconsideration was later given to his case.

Responsible churchmen in Angola have often tried to speak out about existing abuses. If they were successful in seeing high officials (which was not always the case), note would be taken of the abuses, but little was done to correct the situation. In a dictatorial system, no one dares make a decision except the man at the top and he is usually uninterested or too busy.

The Portuguese react strongly to any criticism—as do all of us. However, in a democratic social order, leaders must take criticism, and should profit therefrom. In a dictatorship, those who openly criticize are severely chastised. Was the church ready for the reaction from Lisbon which might mean imprisonment and expulsion of missionaries and even more severe reprisals to nationals? It seemed that finally it was.

In May, 1961, mission headquarters in London, Boston, and New York almost simultaneously released stories and pictures of Portuguese violence in Angola, confirming stories which had leaked from other sources. As expected, the Portuguese reaction was prompt, strong, and at times contradictory. The red herring of communism was raised. ". . . one Cabinet minister in Lisbon implied that Baptists were linked with communism because there is a Baptist pastor in Moscow" (Robert H. Estabrook). Missionaries were accused of collaboration with "terrorists." Some missionaries were imprisoned in Angola and later sent to Lisbon. Some church property was confiscated. Visas for most returning missionaries were denied. More pastors were imprisoned. A public relations firm in the United States was engaged to enhance the Portuguese image and it is reported that a similar measure was taken in London. Articles appeared in magazines upholding the Portuguese. Large packets of free material telling of the atrocities committed in northern Angola at the beginning of the revolt were widely circulated, especially to Methodist and Baptist pastors.

The author wishes to reaffirm his deep conviction that none of the missionaries imprisoned in, or expelled from, Angola has ever been involved in any plans for violence against the Salazar government. They abhor, as do I, the violent methods adopted by Angolan nationalists. They equally repudiate senseless massacres by the white colonists against the defenseless Africans. If we appear to have become the spokesmen for the latter, it is only because they are the more oppressed.

The church in Angola is suffering. Will it survive? Persecution from without has seldom destroyed the church although its normal growth can be greatly impeded. The decision to reveal injustices practiced in Angola was not taken in a spirit of malice or as a reprisal for damage done. It was taken because the Salazar regime in Portugal had gone too far in allowing indignities and brutal treatment of people for whom Christ died. One African pastor, now in prison, surely spoke for many if not all of his fellows when he stated, "The church will rise again, for it still lives in the hearts of the people." As it has been throughout history, the blood of the martyrs again may become the seed of the church.

Part III

THE CHURCH AND ITS FUTURE

A LOOK AHEAD

If the church is to face its future wisely in central and southern Africa, it must commit itself to certain basic attitudes and modes of action:

It must listen attentively to what both God and man would say about its actual condition today—to the vocal, impetuous, largely inexperienced youth, as well as to the conservative, experienced, responsible and sometimes tired segment of the church. Jesus said, ". . . and upon this rock I will build my church" (MATTHEW 16:18). God spoke to Abraham and Samuel; to Moses and Isaiah; to the disciples and Saint Paul; to Francis of Assisi and to Luther; to Calvin and to Wesley; to Pope John—and He speaks to the church in Africa.

The church must react constructively to criticisms and suggestions. The church has been established, but it must be reborn with African features.

The church must assess its resources objectively. Past failures must be studied and the programs from which they arose eliminated; successes need to be used as a foundation for expansion.

The church must seek to know the mind of Christ. As a fellowship which owes its foundation to Jesus Christ, the church of tomorrow must ever seek to know His mind in the changing circumstances of life.

The church must call all to work arduously. The task before all disciples is as impossible as it has always been. The eight-hour day in a forty-hour week is not for those who would be coworkers with God in the re-creation of the church of Christ in Africa. It is an all-the-time job.

The church must plan wisely and cooperatively. Good architects have their roots in the past, are aware of the conditions of the present, and build for the future. Christians can do no less. They must follow Paul in pressing "toward the mark for the prize of the high calling of God in Christ Jesus" (PHILIPPIANS 3:14).

The church must venture forth on faith. Instability surrounds us and insecurity undermines—the time is ripe for vision and for venture! Abraham moved out, not knowing where he was going, but satisfied that he was being led by God (GENESIS 12:1-3). The church in Africa must not let glorious visions fade—let Christ's followers walk confidently into the future!

15

Responsibility

AFRICANS ARE AS talented as, but no more capable than, other people. They have a variety and abundance of gifts, but they also have limitations—as do all members of the human species—and like others, they need training for responsibility in all phases of national, community, and church life.

In this part of Africa there is a tendency to assume that the African is going to fail when given responsibility. "Look at the mess in the Congo!" has become a slogan of disparagement among some Europeans. But where were the *trained* Congolese when independence arrived so unexpectedly and prematurely? The Congo is not so much an example of African failure to produce as of European failure to prepare. The amazing things about Africa today are its nonviolence in achieving independence and its relative success after independence. Fortunately, in most countries, there have been those limited few who have received sufficient training to provide mature and objective leadership. But what of the church?

In that vast area extending from the Atlantic Ocean to the Indian Ocean, and from a few degrees south of the equator to the "great, grey-green, greasy Limopo"—an area half as large as the United States—there are not a dozen Protestant African ministers with university degrees. The author personally knows only four in the area, with a fifth due to return soon. Of the four, one has just been released from prison in Angola; one is in ecumenical, administrative work in Leopoldville; one is in educational work in Katanga; and the fourth is giving full time to politics in Dar-es-Salaam.

A few years ago an international ecumenical team investigated training for the ministry in Africa. After six months' study, they recommended very strongly that the training program be strengthened by establishing ecumenical training centers. These recommendations have been implemented to a large degree, and more recently the Theological Education Fund has made possible additional facilities and an expanded program in a few centers in Africa. Even so, most of these centers are not yet on a par with similar institutions in other parts of the world. Thus, for an African minister to receive training equal to that offered in other countries, the best possibility is a "crash" training program overseas.

Experience shows there is no dearth of suitable candidates when it becomes known that the road to the ministry is not a dead-end street. Many of the more aggressive and ambitious youth, although dedicated to the church, are not willing to offer themselves for subnormal training in Africa when they see other professions gettting full university training; also they sense the tremendous responsibility of the Christian ministry. Consequently, they continue in their teaching or business rather than accept training which will give the ecclesiastical authorities an excuse to keep them in inferior positions in the church, or to place them where their lack of broad and profound training will cause embarrassment and will cast reflection upon their race and vocation.

The call of the African ultranationalists is to return to the religious practices of past years. The call is strong and persistent. No European can stop a movement in that direction simply by preaching against it and calling it godless. A pietistic appeal to devotion to Jesus Christ will not be enough. Perhaps nothing can stop it. It will take more than piety, more than a threat of hell; it will take a knowledge of church and world history, an understanding of both psychology and theology. Above all, it will take an understanding of African culture. It will demand someone keen, with the background to analyze and evaluate both western worship patterns and traditional African practices, and enough prestige to impress the masses.

Because they lack training, most African ministers, sincere and dedicated though they be, cannot counsel youth adequately in our modern society. A high-school student writes, "One of the major issues weakening the church is its African leaders, who have not received enough training and education to help them sufficiently during the operation of their most difficult work. Because this is a period of political confusion and inquiry, the leaders without adequate education will be unable to meet these questions, and by so doing the church loses the confidence of its people, especially the young people."

But guidance *can* be given by those with breadth of knowledge —both of African and European cultures—with clear understanding of the intense drive of the African people for fulfillment, a sympathetic desire to contribute toward their well-being, and a sensitivity to the leading of the Holy Spirit.

Unless African ministers immediately receive training equal in quality to that of their western counterparts, the morning sky will be red with foreboding for the church. But what can be done in the lone hour before the sun rises? A beginning can be made, and if that step is taken now perhaps the African people will stretch their patience a little further to await the time they can hear the gospel preached with authority by their own sons in Oxford English, Coimbra Portuguese, Parisian French, and African dialects.

To quibble over how a well-trained ministry will be supported, or the moral evils in western society to which they will be subjected, or the gap between degree ministers and uneducated parishioners is only adding dry brush to the already roaring fire which threatens to consume the church. A trained African ministry can do that which no westerner can do—build a Christian church in which the religious aspirations of the African people will find fulfillment.

Many talk of a multiracial society and a nonracial church. Yet training continues at two levels: the African ministerial candidates at a post-elementary-school level and the European candidates at the post-university level. How can a multiracial church be built on this basis? There will never be a nonracial society in Africa, within the church or without, until there is equality of training for equal responsibilities. The staff at Epworth

Theological College, near Salisbury, Southern Rhodesia, deserves congratulations for opening an A-stream of training and admitting both Europeans and Africans to the course. This provides hope for a nonracial church in multiracial areas of the continent.

It would be interesting to obtain a list of the degrees from the present heads of the various denominations in this part of Africa. One would find a sprinkling of doctorates, a lot of master's degrees, and a quantity of academic bachelor's degrees and bachelors of theology or divinity. The present leadership of the denominations has been constituted on the basis of qualities of leadership, dedication, and experience—but also because of depth of training. Succession to these high and holy offices requires training commensurate to the responsibility.

What has been said about the ministry holds equally true for all phases of community and national life. There are in every land those rare individuals who are so amply equipped with abilities that they rise to the top and give creative leadership in their business or profession, without training. Still, they are rare. Lest I be accused of focusing on the human to the exclusion of the divine initiative, I would add that God can and does use to His glory all people who love Him. However, this does not negate the main thesis: God uses dedicated, trained people to His *greater* glory.

What can the church do? It is limited in finances—but God is not. If the church can come up with some creative proposals which it will back with conviction and sacrifice, resources can be found.

Conditions differ so greatly in the various countries from the Atlantic to the Indian Oceans that no specific plan will completely fit into the current stage of educational development everywhere. Let us use Southern Rhodesia as an example, with the understanding that adjustments would have to be made in adjacent territories; African education only will be dealt with as European students have much more adequate facilities at the present time.

In all the subcontinent, there is a need for widely expanded preuniversity training. Although the need for more four-year high schools in Southern Rhodesia is recognized, let that be bypassed for the moment in considering the post-four-year-high-school training, beginning with the Cambridge Certificate or its equivalent. In December of 1962, there were 253 African youth who completed four years of high-school training. To gain admission to the local University College, they must have an additional two years of schooling. At present there are only two academic schools where this can be obtained—Fletcher High School and Goromonzi Secondary School. Further, one of the basic requirements for entrance to either of these two government schools is a credit in English. (Each student is graded in each subject: "pass," "credit," or "distinction.") Now it so happens that a student may get "distinction" in all of his other subjects, but if he fails to get a "credit" in English grammar, he is excluded from both of the existing high schools with post Form IV work. Records show that out of the 253 African pupils getting their Cambridge or high-school certificates in December, 1962, only 132 were qualified—because of the English requirement—to enter either Goromonzi or Fletcher High Schools. Out of this 132, only 45 were actually attending these schools in 1963. In the remaining group of high-school graduates, many are highly capable of advanced studies; but, as far as Rhodesia is concerned, there are no further openings that lead to the academic professions. Because English is always a second language for Africans, it is not surprising that they find it more difficult to obtain a "credit" in English than do the European pupils; yet the requirements are the same to "keep the standards high." A new scheme has been organized by the University College of Rhodesia and Nyasaland whereby a pupil may study externally for one year following the Cambridge examination and then attend a special course at the university for another year. After this he *may* be accepted for further academic work. However, at present, the first experimental group is limited to forty students for the three territories of the Federation.

If the churches could unite to establish a Christian Junior College at some central point and accept a hundred of the best-qualified pupils who fail to get a place at the two government schools each year, it would be an invaluable service to humanity in the name of Christ. Special classes in English by trained remedial teachers could bring up the English deficiency in most cases. If the standards were kept high, upon completion of the two-year post-Cambridge course, the students might then be able to continue their training at the University College in Salisbury,

A crash program should be organized to seek funds and scholarships for overseas study at both university and postgraduate levels. (Later it should be limited to the latter only.) The need for trained people in all professions is so great that the present backlog of Cambridge graduates should easily find places in universities in other parts of Africa, in the United States, in India, and in those universities of Europe which require four, rather than six, years of high-school work. Students of intelligence and dedication are available if travel funds and scholarships can be found. Were such a program nonsectarian, help might be solicited for travel from large foundations, scholarships from well-endowed universities, or the cost might have to come from grants.

Something should be done immediately to attract ministerial candidates and train them through the university level. Such a program might be called "priorities for preachers." The ministry *must* keep pace with the rapid development of the countries of southern Africa. If some kind of united approach were made to search out suitable candidates, scholarships might be found through the World Council of Churches, the Theological Education Fund, benevolent organizations—even from already overstrained denominational sources.

Those of the Protestant tradition have a reason for concern as they visualize the Africa of 1990. Cairo already has its great Islamic University. The Roman Catholics have a number of smaller colleges, but reports are that Lovanium, outside Leopoldville, plans on a student body of 7000 by 1970. As far as I know, the only Protestant university on the whole African continent is the comparatively small Cuttington College in Liberia. The Congo Polytechnic Institute is not yet training at the university level nor has the proposed Protestant University at Stanleyville started to function. Even if one or the other should become an established university, the scope is national rather than continental. Isn't it high time for a United Protestantism to establish a great university for the subcontinent? Nothing of local or national dimensions will meet the need; a great multilingual university in the best Protestant tradition is indicated—to provide religious balance and challenge to those of the other faiths already established. Even though not envisaged at the Addis Ababa UNESCO conference, this matter should be given priority rating by the World Council of Churches as it plans for the future of Africa. Such a venture would not only provide Africa with intellectual stimulus, religious undergirding and balance, but would also be a mighty force in uniting Africa politically, and Protestantism religiously.

May God give His church faith and vision for this day, that there may be responsible Christian leadership tomorrow for the church, the nations, and the world!

16

Relinquish the Reins

THE TITLE OF this chapter dates the author; nevertheless, it has meaning for the older generation. Perhaps, for the younger ones, it should be called "Get Out From Behind the Wheel!" or "Turn Over the Controls!"

Although in one or two instances the major denominations attempted to appoint African auxiliary bishops, administrative assistants, presidents of conferences, and secretaries of synods, to a large extent the control of the established churches remains in the hands of Europeans; even in groups temporarily chaired by Africans, the power behind the chair is often European. The local church will never become an indigenous African institution as long as it is administered by Europeans. If the Europeans insist on continued control, as indeed they may, the church as it now exists may gradually fade away. In its place, a new racist or nationalist church more expressive of the emotions and politico-religious aspirations of the African people may be born. This extreme step probably will not be taken *if* the sponsoring denominations, as well as the European leaders in Africa, can see the wisdom of the immediate transfer of authority. It will come eventually; to delay will cause the world church immeasurable harm.

The denominations which are truly multiracial in their composition are in an extremely difficult position today because the European segment of their membership views African leadership with disfavor and the African constituency disdains continued European control. These denominations will undoubtedly attempt a solution (which for a few years may be somewhat artificial), such as alternating positions of leadership between Africans and Europeans. Ultimately they must all be willing to choose the best person for the position regardless of race. That should be the ideal in all denominations; but, because of the paucity of trained Africans, a policy of forced leadership may be advisable. There are pros and there are cons.

There are five chief reasons why the transfer of administrative responsibility should be made *now*.

First: There is the need for experience in administration. Few wise administrators begin to make changes as soon as they take over responsibility. They like to get the feel of office, gain the confidence of their followers, study the need for and effect of possible change, determine their goals and how to attain them. It is quite evident that major changes should be made in the life of the church in Africa, and that they should be made as soon as possible. These changes are such that they must be envisaged and brought about largely by African leaders. Time is of the essence—politically within the nation and *also* religiously within the church. To resist change because of a lack of adequately trained personnel may well be more disastrous than to place inadequately trained people into positions of leadership. The important thing is that a beginning must be made *now* in giving African leaders the experience they need.

Second: With its history of leadership in Africa, the church cannot—at this time of rapid transition—withdraw from the movement which it has set in motion. It will seem somewhat strange if, after producing leaders for the nations, it cannot produce responsible people for its own administration. If you look across Africa, you will see that the great majority of African political leaders have come up through the church. Is the church more adept at training political leaders than spiritual ones? *I* think not. Africans have been slower in pushing their way into positions of church administration than into politics because there has been a very real devotion to their church leaders. The loyal African constituency does not wish to give offense to their present leaders by removing them from their positions, or by deserting them. This sympathetic consideration has not existed to the same degree within the political field. It is therefore all the more urgent that church bodies sense this reticence and graciously make change possible without pressure.

Third: The transfer of authority to indigenous leadership is certainly a pattern within the mainstream of the Christian tradition, and will undoubtedly hasten development in the church, as it has in the political field. Local resources will be tapped more quickly and deeply under African leadership than under European. Had the African people been in decision-making positions years ago, there would be more trained churchmen now. There is something about responsibility which brings forth the best in individuals and in groups—the challenge of a job is a tremendously sharp spur to attainment.

Fourth: The life of much of the church in Africa has been imposed by foreigners and may for that reason be considered artificial. A fairly adequate and secure foundation has been laid, but to that has been added much that will not endure under local conditions after European support is withdrawn. A process of adaptation of the ideas of the west is constantly taking place. Part of the superstructure will be pulled down and replaced by elements more in keeping with the local environment. It may be an advantage for that to happen soon, so that a permanent superstructure which will appeal to the majority can be constructed. If this must be done (and I think it is inevitable), the sooner the better!

Fifth: "What is the Holy Spirit saying to the church today?" If God's Spirit is leading in this direction, then the church must respond or betray the Master. There may be those who do not feel the leading of the Spirit in relinquishing power and responsibility to the African people. Perhaps we should then ask, "Is the present leadership of the church conscious that God's Spirit is urging them to retain their positions?" The church *must* move at the impulse of His love without thought of position or prestige. There is nothing more important that can be done at this time than to seek the leading of the Holy Spirit in this matter.

So much for the factors favoring changeover of leadership; now for the "cons." Those who argue *against* fairly rapid turnover of responsibility for the administration of church affairs point out quickly that responsibility is not something which can be *given*—it must be *assumed.* At the present time there are few Africans qualified by training and experience to move into positions of authority. However, shouldn't the church follow the example of Jesus and give responsibility a little before the people are ready for it?—trusting the Holy Spirit to provide the necessary wisdom?

Many people argue rightly that the church is supranational and consequently it should not matter who is in a position of authority. They say the church should not become purely African and nationalistic; therefore, they seek to avoid that danger by retaining European leadership. This position is reasonable if it is the constituency of the church in Africa which selects such leadership instead of having it imposed from the outside.

Another argument against the transfer of authority is that considerable financial help for the ongoing program comes from overseas. Will the supporting agencies be willing to have funds administered by non-Europeans? It is to be hoped that supporting societies are not so narrow-minded or so unbelieving that they do not trust the Holy Spirit to give guidance to an African-led church just as much as to one administered by Europeans. The concern of many in this respect is lack of training and experience rather than lack of natural ability and personal integrity of African colleagues.

One must admit, regretfully, that in all probability funds from overseas will diminish with the withdrawal of European leadership from church administration. It is only natural that Europeans, sent by their own denominational agencies, have closer relationships with their supporting churches than will Africans. Most missionaries spend the greater part of their furloughs telling about the needs in Africa and encouraging the churches of their homelands to give. Sending and supporting agencies must maintain their interest in the church in Africa regardless of who may be in top administrative positions. We hope that missionaries will continue to serve and enrich the life of the church even when they do not direct its activities! It is natural to expect that the increase in local interest will ultimately offset any overseas slump; it should be so, and church history will verify the fact that this often happens.

A very real concern among those who hesitate to hand over the reins is that there may be a considerable slump in moral discipline. The standard of conduct will probably undergo a change —this change may be less western, but there is no assurance that it will be less Christian!

Church leaders argue also that in the church, as in the political field, Europeans are not ready to accept African leadership. That is true of many, but certainly not of all. If the church has the courage to select African leaders, the public in general will accept them. Those responsible for truly multiracial churches may have to decide wherein lies the greater loss: in the exit of a few Europeans or many Africans.

In *Africa—What Lies Ahead,* D. K. Chisiza, Parliamentary Secretary of the Ministry of Finance in Nyasaland, warns, "There must be an accelerated transfer of responsibility to Africans. The alternative is to hang onto leadership against which there is growing disfavor and see impressive congregations dwindle to tiny clusters of doubtful adherents."

17

The Burden

EVEN WHEN AN African is in the driver's seat, there will be a need to share the burdens of developing the church. I hope that the church in Africa will be supranational and supraracial —that it will be an integral part of the world-wide church. There will be need for continued fellowship forever, and for continued assistance for many years. In like manner, the church in Africa will increase her sharing of ideas and resources with churches in other parts of the world. The church must be mindful of the fact that we are "workers together with God" at all times and in all places.

There are at least three areas in which the western church must continue to share with the church in Africa. *First*—through a continuing exchange of ideas via world conferences and united programs. The essentially universal life of the church must be maintained. The continuous flow of ideas for stimulation and cross-fertilization must be intensified. International church conferences must come to Africa to make an impact on the life of the continent. Africa must be more adequately represented on committees of the World Council of Churches and at interdenominational and denominational meetings. Much is already being done; much more *should* be done to bring Africans into the very center of the life of the church universal.

Second—through the need for continued financial sharing for many years ahead. Although there is vast wealth in Africa, much of it is still unexploited; Africa is so underdeveloped that great stress will be placed on national development. The tremendous urgency to raise the economic level of the people may result in the real danger that one aspect of national development—that of the church—will be overlooked. The economy of the average church member is so low that he simply cannot carry the full financial load of the church in its present European garb, with its many and varied arms of service, until he himself prospers. Therefore, support will have to continue from overseas, if the effective services are to continue.

The fear that overseas funds will be sharply reduced or cut off immediately causes many thoughtful Africans to move slowly in their insistence that needed administrative changes be made now. We *must not* allow the sharing of resources from afar to cease abruptly. The church in Africa (out of fear of curtailment of overseas funds) should not be hamstrung in deciding to do what is timely and right.

The sharing process is as needed in the more affluent areas of the world as it is in the underdeveloped—if the "sending" churches cease to care about the needs of others, they will become dead institutions.

Third—there is a need for the continued sharing of personnel. Many missionaries have a fear that as the church moves into indigenous leadership, their services will no longer be needed. There is no sustained move on the part of the African church people to oust all missionaries; on the contrary, as responsibilities are gradually turned over, there is a growing appreciation of the burdens which the missionaries have carried for years.

More and more Africans speak appreciatively of missionaries who sense the new day and are willing to adjust to it. One high-school pupil wrote, "Missionaries are needed now more than ever before. This time of change needs those who have a strong Christian faith to encourage, advise, and even rebuke. . . ."

Mr. Chisiza made it emphatic that missionaries are wanted: ". . . transfer of responsibility does not imply the return of foreign missionaries back to Europe, America, or wherever they came from. If anything, it necessitates their presence. The Africans who will take over will need to be initiated into the traditions of patience, devotion, perseverance, and routine work. They will need the technical know-how which the foreign missionaries possess. They will need the company of foreign missionaries to broaden their outlook."

Even Africans who are very critical of present relationships between missionaries and non-Europeans admit that the missionary is needed. One high-school pupil wrote, "The concept that the African was working *for* the missionary must have its funeral. There should be the feeling that the African and the missionary are working together towards one common goal." A more mature student, now in India, wrote, "Most certainly missionaries are needed . . . they must be fully interested in the people they serve and sincerely appreciate and seek to build upon any good aspects of the African traditions. They must acknowledge and demonstrate the fact that all men are equal in the sight of God. They must be genuinely enthusiastic about developing African leadership and be happy to work under deserving African leadership. . . . The missionaries must acknowledge and recognize the infinite, boundless, and limitless capacities of an African as an equal member of the human family and must endeavor to develop such capacities so that in due course, the contributions and interdependence of the African and the white race will be reciprocal."

The modern missionary to Africa is needed because missionaries will always be needed to share their faith in Jesus Christ. The main purpose of the whole missionary movement is that He might be known and that His teachings might be understood. As a group, missionaries are second to none in their dedication to Jesus Christ, in their willingness to sacrifice for the extension of His Kingdom, in their optimism that God's purpose will prevail, in the courage to follow their inner convictions and to be led aright by the Holy Spirit. The qualities which they possess are needed in the church everywhere.

He is needed because missionary specialists are badly needed to enrich the life of the church. If only the absolutely necessary functions can be performed and the bare framework of the program maintained, there is little opportunity to add that which gives real meaning and enrichment. If missionaries can be replaced in the routine administrative positions they now hold, they can better use their specialized training in adding more content to the established program and in developing such new fields as music, art, drama, literature, spiritual healing, and cultural research.

The missionary is needed to help keep the church in Africa universal. With the pressures of pan-Africanism, there is a very real danger that the church might become too provincial. I firmly believe that this has happened to some of the numerous separatist groups in the southern part of the continent. The presence of an "outsider" often keeps people from taking an extreme position. The presence of "expatriates," as missionaries are sometimes called, will tend to keep the church in Africa supranational.

Finally, missionaries, with their years of experience and stability of character, are needed to take up the slack which will inevitably come while Africans are gaining experience in administration. Mistakes will be made and scapegoats will be needed. Corrections must be made; messes must be cleaned up—not a very attractive task, to be sure, but one in which the missionary can serve effectively, if he will. Because others had to do these things for him when he was inexperienced, the missionary may be willing to help his African brethren on their way to maturity.

The new day in Africa may call for a new type of missionary recruit. The physical hazards of past years are seldom present today, but the spiritual and psychological demands have greatly increased. In the future more and more emphasis should be placed on the qualities which the church in Africa thinks important in the missionaries who are sent. The function of determining who comes in the first place, and who remains, must increasingly be the prerogative of the church in Africa. The sending agencies might well consider carefully the following qualifications when selecting missionaries:

1) The missionary must be as free from self as possible, with a deep dedication to do the will of God. He cannot easily teach those qualities of life which he himself does not possess. If there is to be a church that moves at the divine impulse, all church workers must possess that quality themselves. There is no substitute for complete self-surrender to the will of God. Only those who seek the divine will in their every act should come, or will remain in Africa. The glamour period of missions—the romantic era—is over, and only he who has the inner stamina of a divine call will be able to withstand the demands being made today.

2) The missionary in Africa must be flexible. In a constantly changing environment, rigidity will cause the strongest character to break. So much of life is gray—the good and bad are so intermingled, the demands for change are so constant and the compromise so impelling—that the inflexible individual will snap under the strain.

3) A winsome personality is urgently needed. Most Europeans are now suspect in southern Africa. The personality of the missionary may determine whether he will be accepted or rejected. Is he outgoing? Will he extend a helping hand readily? Will he smile with his eyes as well as show his teeth? Is there depth of conviction and sincerity to give urgency to his words of unwanted advice? Is there a natural warmth of personality? Does he have a sense of humor?

4) Complete sincerity is always an asset in Christian work, or in any other profession. It is an imperative in modern Africa. No missionary candidate who is not completely sincere with himself, with his colleagues, and with his God, should seek service overseas. The African is a naturally keen psychologist—reads character like an open book. Woe to the missionary who tries to bluff, whose words are shallow, whose smile is unnatural, whose hospitality is forced! If the missionary motivation is unworthy, the secret will out. If he is fleeing an unbearable situation in his homeland, he will need to flee further than Africa.

5) Sharing is an admirable quality which the African culture rates highly. Motives are always mixed, but there must be a willingness to share with others the gifts which God has bestowed upon us if one is to survive in Africa. He who regards his assets selfishly will have a rough time. There is little place for the egocentric life in African society. The call to Africa is a call to self-giving, a call to sharing, a call to sacrifice. He who builds a protective wall around himself will find cold isolation. He who gives of himself will find warm responsive fellowship.

6) Let no one come to Africa who is not secure in his own environment. Modern Africa is critical—especially of the white man. The waters undermine, the sun burns, the wind chafes, the mosquitoes bite, and the cold stare challenges. Africa is no place for the person who is less than well adjusted at home. The traditionally benighted African has become defiant. He will welcome

those who have adequate spiritual qualifications and who can produce—provided they are willing to do so on a basis of equality in a growing, competitive society.

7) Humility is the gift appreciated above all. The African is so fed up with the arrogant European that he will reject any individual who shows a domineering attitude. The modern African has a growing consciousness of his place in the world: he is a child of God. He refuses to accept anyone with an attitude of superiority, be it in the realm of the spiritual, social or cultural aspects of life. But he who comes as a child—to learn as well as to teach—will find a warm welcome.

8) The person who comes to Africa must be well grounded in his faith. He must know in whom he believes, as well as what he believes. A simple but deep faith is convincing. It is a shield when the petrol bombs are thrown. It is a comfort behind prison bars. It provides courage when the lion roars, or the government tries to intimidate.

9) A missionary should come to Africa with a keen sensitivity to the feelings of others. The antennae of our lives must be attuned to the spiritual wave-lengths of our associates. He who would serve acceptably must sense the feelings of others and respond warmly, wisely, and winsomely.

All of these qualities are not commonly found in any one individual—rarely are they found in any one missionary! Thus it behooves the modern missionary in Africa to be prepared to accept criticism, to apply it if it is relevant, and to grow to a more perfect maturity. This ability to learn as one lives is most essential.

As a pilgrim of the way, a missionary must welcome guidance and, having been guided, help those who are seeking the way along with him. Let him not hesitate to come to Africa; he is needed—to share his faith, his ideals, his knowledge, his experience.

18

Cultural Values

TRADITIONAL AFRICAN CULTURE was neither all bad nor all good; there were positive factors which held the culture together and negative factors which degraded human personality or destroyed life. Certain elements in African culture (as it remains today) are positive and should be retained, and other elements are negative and should be discarded. The problem lies in evaluating the partially good and the partially bad. It is here that the decision must be left to those who are a part of the culture—only they can determine whether the overall effect will be positive or negative.

The various elements of African culture may be divided into four groups (if one realizes that in life no such rigid division is possible): arts and crafts, communion with the saints, psychological forces, and "the common good" as a sociological factor.

There is still much to be learned about the origin of certain trades; evidence of prehistoric craftmanship is found in the Zimbabwe Ruins near Fort Victoria, so-called slave pits and irrigation ditches in Inyanga Mountain area, and in other places. Certainly at some period, before records were kept, there were very clever artisans living in the southern part of the continent.

There are herbalists, some of whom—though largely self-taught or through apprenticeship—have considerable knowledge of botany and are well versed in the properties of various plants. These men have learned their secrets from their predecessors and they guard their secrets carefully. Undoubtedly they have knowledge which should be conserved and shared for the benefit of humanity. On March 18, 1963, the *Rhoderis Herald* carried an article entitled " 'BUSH DOCTORS' ASKED TO SHARE SECRETS" which indicates that the world is becoming increasingly aware of these values. It states:

> Uganda's "bush doctors" who carry out home cures with traditional herbs, soils, and drugs, have been asked to share their secrets with the rest of the world. Health Minister Dr. E.N.S. Lumu said last night that the Government is starting an investigation of "native medicine" in order to find out the efficacy of the old methods before the passage of time obliterates them. The Minister assured the medicos that none of their secrets would be revealed without permission.

Certain crafts such as smelting and iron-working have largely disappeared except in the more isolated areas. Weaving, basket-making, and similar crafts are still practiced, but decreasingly so. Combed thatching, though it makes a beautiful roof, is rapidly disappearing. Carving and sculpture is taking on new life with the influx of tourists and the opening of overseas markets. The detailed work seen on old stools and chiefs' staffs is seldom found today; but in general there is a growing demand for African artifacts, including painting, which is being encouraged by contemporary artists in the western world who see in it great power and originality.

Probably the greatest near-loss has been African music, and it is precisely this art which may have the most meaning for the church. Sporadic but serious attempts are being made to collect, study, classify, and reintroduce African music into the worship of the church. However, the attempts often meet with considerable resistance, especially from the older generation of African clergymen. Since a majority of Africans find emotional expression in music and have a natural gift for it, it is time that the church came out in favor of the use of traditional music and art in worship. A Mindolo study group* recommended that "high value should be placed upon such folk-tune hymn singing as arises spontaneously and readily establishes itself in people's hearts. Genuine African cultural forms should be sought for basic liturgical elements from the church's history." As in everything else there will have to be careful evaluation and selection.

* In September of 1962, the World Council of Churches sponsored a consultation of thirty-five church leaders (twenty were Africans) at the Mindolo Ecumenical Foundation in Kitwe, Northern Rhodesia.

Most Africans have a persistent longing to retain communication with departed members of their family, clan, or social group. In the Mindolo reports so far released is the comment:

> African ancestor cults, as a part of these world-views, have been rejected by western missionaries, but they have found recognition in some of the independent churches, while many African members of older churches also adhere to traditional belief and ritual relating to the ancestors. . . . To stimulate fresh thinking over the whole range of ideas involved, the churches should become involved in a serious dialogue between the traditional world-view and the continuing revelation of Jesus Christ through the Scriptures. . . . Where cults and beliefs have been driven into secrecy through denunciation or disciplinary action, an atmosphere of confidence first needs to be restored. It is possible that traditional forms of ritual may be adapted, given new content, and so renewed.

It is possible that the western world's scientific approach may have overlooked a very important field of communication between the living and the spirits of the deceased. Because it has such meaning to the African people, and in its own search for truth, the church should permit, and even encourage, continued experimentation.

Revelation through dreams and visions is common in the Scriptural records as well as in Africa. Although they are not considered as the highest means of revelation of God to man by Biblical scholars, there is no reason why they should be discouraged. Often a call to the Christian ministry has come in the form of a dream or vision. This form of revelation is very meaningful to most Africans.

The gift of prophecy has not been encouraged in the modern western church. Yet prophecy served a very useful end in the Old Testament period. The great movement toward the church in West Africa, following the travels and utterances of the Prophet Harris, is well known. Prophecy certainly is within the scope of Christian tradition and should not be overly restricted in the life of the church. At the same time, it must be remembered that false prophets have caused—and can cause—considerable damage to people, even in modern times.

The use of psychic phenomena is fairly common in Africa. No

one will ever know how many thousands of people in Africa have died because of suggestion and the use of psychological forces. Many have been cured by the combined power of suggestion, positive thinking, and faith—in the western scientific world, psychological factors are encouraged as a supplement to medicine! In some cases, it has been effective when modern medicine has failed. The Mindolo group reported:

> It is obvious that the ministry of ("faith") healing forms a central part of the life of many independent churches. Western medicine is, as yet, unavailable on any large scale in much of Africa. However, despite the devoted work of many mission hospitals, it often seems divorced from the African's understanding of God's healing relationship with man. While recognizing certain dangers in their approach, we have seen that healing in the independent churches stresses the reality of the spiritual world, the basic unity of man, and the profound inter-relationship of religion and healing, in a way which has met the previously unsatisfied needs of many African Christians. . . . There is . . . a challenge to the old churches in Africa to join churches in other parts of the world in praying for the renewal of the gifts of healing and exorcism by such means as prayer and the laying on of hands.

The values in African family structure and relationships have been badly misunderstood by the church. Traditionally there has been a definite and concentrated effort to work toward a common good. It must be recognized that the common good was usually for a limited group and was not in any sense universal. We must admit also that many cruelties were practiced (such as the killing of twins and, in times of famine, the aged) because of the lack of understanding. But, within the prescribed group, there was a sense of solidarity which gave meaning to life. Sharing within the group was expected and practiced. Widows were either allowed to remain widows under the protection of the group or were given to a brother of the deceased husband. In the interest of the common good, a polygamous system developed so that no woman would be deprived of a family. Up to puberty, there was considerable sexual laxity, but at the beginning of adolescence, the mores were strictly enforced. In order to ensure the stability of family life, an exchange of gifts took place between the two families concerned in marriage. There was a carefully worked-out and strictly enforced system of social ethics. The western social-ethical system which accompanied the church to Africa as part of the gospel has often been in conflict with the African ethic. The church must clarify its position on these and other issues.

Is it more Christian to have organized prostitution, marital infidelity treated with impunity, a rapidly growing divorce rate, and increasing numbers of illegitimate children, than polygamy? Is it more Christian for young women to become prostitutes, call girls, or mistresses than to become the second or third wife of a respected member of the community? Is a socialist government pension scheme more Christian than clan solidarity and common sharing? Is permitting youth to choose their own mates necessarily more Christian than an agreement between families? Is a widow any better or happier in the world alone, than living intimately with a member of her husband's family? Jesus seems to have acceded to the Old Testament custom on this point (MATTHEW 22:24; MARK 12:19; LUKE 20:28).

It is difficult for one who is not a member of a society to evaluate fully its social practices in the light of the gospel. One can fairly well evaluate the practices within his own culture, but even there all do not agree. To condemn the social practices of another group just because they are different from our own is not in keeping with the best interpretation of the gospel. After calling attention to the traditionally negative attitude of the church toward African family life, the Mindolo group noted:

> In respect of this issue, a loveless, censorious, and legalistic approach has developed which does not reflect the spirit of our Lord Jesus. The church is called to be a minister of Christ's redeeming power and grace, not His punitive instrument. In the judgment of many of us, the polygamous status of a new convert from a non-Christian background should be no barrier to his acceptance into church membership.

I am not prepared to recommend that the church accept the

traditional social practices into its life or to affirm that the church has been right in rejecting them. But certainly elements of value should be retained, and it is largely the enlightened African Christians who must decide these practices which have value. This will call for concentrated study, meditation, and thought.

The problem is further complicated by inability to know what the future will bring. Were certain African traditional practices to be approved by the church, would this mean that the strong social discipline of former times could be brought back and applied to eliminate evil influences from the west? I think not. Africa has changed. One cannot turn back to compare and evaluate the traditional African culture of a hundred years ago with current western practices. Time moves forward, not backward. Therefore, the most feasible solution is to bring the light of the gospel to play upon various social practices to establish their harm or value.

19

The Gospel

CHRISTIANITY IS OFTEN thought of as the religion of the Bible. This is especially true for Protestants; Roman Catholics place a greater emphasis on tradition than do Protestants, but even they appear to be turning more and more to the Bible as their basis of authority. In another very real sense, the teachings of Protestantism and Roman Catholicism alike are based on the life and utterances of Jesus Christ, the God-Man. Without Christ as the central figure, Christianity would not exist. It is He who founded the church (MATTHEW 16:18); it is He who chose the first disciples and taught them His doctrine (MATTHEW 10:1-5); it is He who commissioned them to go forth and evangelize throughout the whole world (MATTHEW 28:18-20); it is He who promised the Comforter, even the Holy Spirit, to abide with His followers forever (JOHN 16:7).

Christianity is the religion based on the teachings of Christ. In seeking a basis for Christian belief and an authority for Christian actions, one goes first to the words and deeds of Jesus, as set forth in the four gospels. Following that (for understanding and encouragement) are the letters to the early churches, and then one goes to the Old Testament for the background of Judaism out of which Christianity developed.

Has the teaching of the church in Africa been too centered in the negative "thou shalt not's" of the Old Testament rather than in the positive "thou shalt's" of the New Testament? Has too much attention been paid to keeping the "questionables" out of the church? or to expelling the "undesirables"?—not enough placed on going out into the highways and byways and compelling the "whosoevers" to come in? Has too much preaching been *against* sin and not enough *for* holiness? too much about death and not enough about life? too much about hell and not enough about heaven? too much about the Ten Commandments and not enough about the new commandment of love (JOHN 13:34)?

If one goes through the gospels carefully, trying to find those values which motivated Jesus during His brief ministry upon earth, three will stand out: the supreme value of the human personality; the importance of service in finding meaning to life; and the place of solitude, reflection, prayer and worship in finding strength for service.

Without doubt, man's system of values in life is reflected more by what he does than by what he says. One's ideals are more nearly mirrored by his actions than by his utterances. By *watching* a man, one may discover his true set of values; from *listening* to him, one may discover the accepted mores of his social group. Deeds show our true personal values; words may reproduce artificial or superficial values which have been imposed upon us, but which are not our own. If one would learn the true nature and values of a man, follow him, live with him. If a man is utterly sincere, there will not be any discrepancy between his deeds and his words.

For Jesus, there was no value of greater significance than human personality, any personality. Jesus spent much of His time encouraging, instructing, and re-establishing persons. The freeing of the demoniac was important, even though a herd of swine was lost (MATTHEW 8:28-32). It was more important that His hungry disciples be fed than that the law of the sabbath be upheld (MATTHEW 12:1). Is it any wonder that Jesus, with His interest in people, cured the man by the pool of Bethzatha even though it was on the sabbath (JOHN 5:2-8, RSV)? Or that He reacted similarly to the blind man by the pool of Siloam (JOHN 9:16)? People, all people, were the maximum concern of Jesus, not the observance of certain rituals and laws—and so it must be for His followers in Africa and elsewhere.

The service impulse seemed to provide Jesus with considerable motivation, if we are to judge by His numerous deeds of compassion. His tender-heartedness toward all people so impressed the writers of the gospels that they mentioned His deeds of mercy and healing more than any other one function. John makes mention of five specific cases of healing; Luke, the doctor, mentions Jesus' alleviation of suffering at least nineteen times; Mark, eighteen times; and Matthew, sixteen times. If one reads the New Testament carefully, the healing ministry of Jesus seems to be at least as noteworthy as His preaching or teaching ministry. Does this say anything to the church in Africa?

One cannot get away from the fact that Jesus spent a major portion of His time and energy serving people. Some may have followed Him for the loaves and fishes; but, the important thing is that they followed. People everywhere go where they receive help. Jesus' ministry was highly spiritual but He recognized that man is more than spirit, and He dealt with man in his totality; because His ministry was a *total* ministry, they listened to Him gladly.

One must also be impressed by the fact that Jesus often withdrew from the multitude for prayer, reflection, meditation, and worship. There are at least nineteen such references in the gospels. The isolation of the mountains, the refreshing burbling of water at the spring, the quiet morning in cathedral or thatched chapel are no luxuries. For those who are constantly giving out, there *must* be a time of spiritual intake, of physical re-creation, of mental re-evaluation. To put it bluntly, if Jesus Himself—who did not feel it was boastful to declare that He and the Father were one—often felt that He needed to renew and replenish His own resources so that He would have more to give to others, how can anyone get along without it? Periodically, man needs a total rehabilitation which comes from God, who can and does rehabilitate, refresh, re-energize, and re-create.

Most of the gospel teachings are positive. Their range covers most of the relationships of life. Often they deal with attitudes instead of detailed instructions regarding specific problems. A central theme, were one word to be chosen, probably would be "*love.*" ". . . God so loved the world that he gave . . ." (JOHN 3:16). "Greater love hath no man than this, that a man lay down his life for his friends" (JOHN 15:13, KJV). "Love your enemies, bless them that curse you, do good to them that hate you, and pray for them which despitefully use you, and persecute you" (MATTHEW 5:44, KJV). "A new commandment I give unto you, That ye love one another" (JOHN 13:34, KJV).

Certainly no passage in the gospels is more meaningful than Jesus' summary of the law, "Thou shalt love the Lord thy God with all thy heart, and with all thy soul, and with all thy mind" (MATTHEW 22:37, KJV). ". . . and with all thy strength," adds Mark (MARK 12:30, KJV). "This is the first and great commandment. And the second is like unto it, Thou shalt love thy neighbour as thyself. On these two commandments hang all the law and the prophets" (MATTHEW 22:38–40, KJV).

Man is not a law unto himself; he has social responsibilities. He who loves not, knows not God; for God is love. (1 JOHN 4:8). Love and service cannot be separated. He who loves, serves; he who serves not, loves not. Love is two-dimensional: first, love for God the Creator Father; and second, love for our neighbors. In order that He would not be misunderstood, Jesus gave an interpretation of neighborliness which once and for all established its inclusiveness (LUKE 10:33). Love for God leads automatically into fields of service.

As the church in Africa struggles to maintain a Christian ethic for her cultural background—a driving motivation for existence —one must bear in mind the central teachings of the gospels rather than any peripheral, western cultural appendages. Above all, it is important that Christ be made known so that His mind can direct the struggling church as it tries to find a foundation which, while African, is nonetheless Christian.

It is none too early for the church in the subcontinent of Africa to recapture the mood of outreach, the expectancy of success, the thrill of rebirth. The missionary movement established in the nineteenth century was one of urgency. Somewhere along the way, the enthusiasm and the urgency have evaporated The missionaries tried to pass the torch on to African evangelists, but in many cases it has been a second-hand enthusiasm without much life. The church in Africa must take the initiative and become more actively evangelistic. This does not mean more departments of evangelism must be set up or that more teams of special evangelists must be sent out. It does mean that the Christian people within Africa must become convinced of the importance of the gospel message.

The question of methodology is involved but it is not all-important. Evangelism is more a mood—a spirit, an attitude, a sharing—than a question of methods. The church must not wait for elaborate preparation, high pressure methods, or world-renowned evangelists. God can use mass evangelism, newspaper appeals, film portrayals, and any other medium; but, the more impersonal the witness, the weaker the impact. The most effective kind of evangelism is personal witnessing to the grace of God in the human heart.

When you tell another what God has done for *you*, he becomes convinced. When he passes along to his neighbors the news of what God has done for *him*, both he and they are blessed.

The western evangelistic approach is individualistic in the main; but the basic African approach is communal. Where tribal patterns have broken down—especially in urban situations where people are cut off from their old communal habits and have accepted some western patterns—the church should strive to win individuals through all the media available, never forgetting that it is the personal testimony: "We have found . . . the Christ!" (JOHN 1:41, KJV) which has the greatest impact both on individuals and on groups.

I have witnessed individual decisions and group decisions—each has had equal permanency. As a young missionary in Angola, I saw a great tribal movement to the church in the Dembos area; in some villages up to ninety per cent of the adults sought Christian baptism and church membership. They have remained loyal to the church. They have been as deeply consecrated as others who have made individual decisions. They have grown in grace and knowledge of Jesus Christ, just as all committed individuals must grow.

From those who have traditionally acted as a group, one should expect communal decisions and give God the praise. It may sometimes be more effective, when a school child has been won to Christ, to say to him, "Go back to your home and win your family; bring them all to Christ and we will receive the whole family into the church." The members of that family can give each other tremendous moral support. The decision of a chief to become Christ's disciple can motivate a whole tribe. When a family, a village, or a whole clan makes a group decision, they can uphold each other wonderfully. One lone Christian convert, struggling to live by his new vision, is much more likely to fall by the wayside than a group all trying together.

With the exception of Portuguese areas of influence and the Sudan, the doors are wide open throughout the subcontinent for evangelism. In the northern two-thirds of Mozambique, there is practically no Protestant witness. The same is partially true of the great southeasterly section of Angola; even there the doors may some day open for a great evangelical thrust into these heretofore sparsely evangelized areas of Africa, and the church should be marshaling her forces now for that thrust.

The immediate future in many African countries is uncertain, but it is in times of uncertainty that the gospel has special meaning—the gospel drives out all fear, replacing it with trust and confidence. Racial hatreds are becoming more intense—what a time for a gospel of love! Selfish interests seem to permeate every transaction—What an antidote is the gospel of sharing and sacrificial giving! What a time for a strong evangelistic proclamation of the whole gospel!

To prepare for the influx following such a proclamation, the church should follow six steps. *First*, seek an *infilling of God's Spirit* which purifies. The smoldering embers within the church need to be fanned again to cleansing heat. There is dross within the church which must be burned away. Africans are accustomed to waiting; an exercise in waiting expectantly for the Holy Spirit would not be amiss. A new Pentecost would set the church afire for God.

Second, from such an infilling of the Spirit will come a *passion that motivates to action*. From the beginning of the Christian era, the outgoing concern for others has inspired people to witness for Jesus Christ. Through witnessing, God's glory has shone through human frailties and other hearts have been touched. Before the influx can possibly come, there must be a *renewal from within* the church itself. When the existing church is revived and renewed through the agonizing spiritual birth-pangs of re-creation, then the influx will come. There must be a warmth of fellowship within the church to receive new converts. They will come when the church is prepared to receive them.

Once they are within, they must be *nurtured by love* that redeems. Initial redemption is through Jesus Christ, but redemption must also be continuous through the redeeming love of the Christian fellowship. I would not humanize the great divine act of redemption made by Jesus Christ once and for all upon the cross; still, in a very real sense, all Christians are called to the cross to participate vicariously in the redemptive act. It is this symbol of the cross and the personal sacrifice made there that binds all Christians together. It is this fellowship of suffering which provides continuous redemption within the body of the church. Without it there will not be the bond that unites or the spirit that sanctifies.

There must be preparation by *corporate worship that disciplines*. As the babe in Christ is nurtured by love, he will grow rapidly. Soon there will have to be discipline. That discipline cannot come from a negative fear of expulsion, but must come from an undergirding of fellowship and group worship. In a very real sense we are of one another. When one member suffers, the whole body suffers (I CORINTHIANS 12:26). A church leader visiting Africa recently said that, as a fellow Christian, he suffered with the African District Superintendent who was driving him about and who could not find any respectable place to eat. Naturally, such identification with this fellow Christian could not help winning the affection of the African District Superintendent. This sympathetic visitor went so far as to say that he considered himself partly responsible for much of the suffering in Africa, even though he has never served on this continent. Christians must undergird and discipline each other in every situation. In the church, in corporate acts of worship, Christians fortify each other and thus exercise a spiritual discipline which is positive and strong. The church lives through creative undergirding rather than by negative separation and expulsion of offenders.

In order that growth may continue, *a challenging task must be provided*. One of the major weaknesses of the church in Africa is that it does not give people—new people—jobs to do.

Often the deacons, the stewards, the local preachers, the Sunday school superintendents are of the 1900 vintage. They have carried their tasks well for many years. May God give them grace to step aside and guide those of two generations later who should be learning churchmanship! (This applies not only to the church in Africa!) An assignment within the fellowship gives one an immediate sense of belonging. The church in Africa would feel new life and strength if there could be a change in ranks. There are tasks for all, but those of my generation must learn to step aside for more creative minds and stronger arms or, at least, they must learn to share more fully with their younger colleagues. This is a difficult lesson for Africa to learn because over the years a great respect for age and experience has been built up. It is that experience which must exercise wisdom by bringing youth to the fore and giving responsible tasks to each.

The church needs to bestir itself now, for the times are favorable. African people are not embarrassed by the mention of religion; they realize that it is a part of the whole of life—like sex—and it does not cause a flush of embarrassment. They are ready to discuss religion as they travel along the road, under a tree, or in a city shop.

The church must forcefully reject any insinuation that it has not made any impact upon Africa and has not contributed to the well-being of its people. The church has made mistakes but there is no cause for undue shame. There *is* reason for every Christian to stand erect, head high, and proclaim in a clear voice the Good News of salvation. Arrogance, conceit, and ostentatious airs are not called for; but a simple, courageous proclamation of faith in the goodness of God should be every Christian's habit.

One must never forget that the Great Commission is for all time and for all people. God, with all His power, operates through individuals of all races and nations. The spread of the gospel should know no barriers, either personal or cultural. All too long the gospel has been preached by Europeans to Africans; let Africans now take the initiative and boldly proclaim the gospel to Europeans, to Asians, and to the people of Mars—should they also come to Africa!

20

Reconciliation

HOSTILITY HAS REACHED a point in Africa today where some do not *want* to be reconciled. School boys may be reconciled while still in the classroom, but once the fists are flying on the playground, it becomes a more difficult task. The church *must* reconcile; it was born of the supreme act of reconciliation between God and man.

Where no common ground exists, the church must try to create at least a little mound of common understanding. Experience over many years of dealing with critical and explosive situations has taught me that if Christian people sincerely desire to know and follow the mind of Christ, an acceptable solution can always be found. Most difficulties arise because so-called Christians do not want to know what the gospel has to say about the problems of life; they are not flexible enough to search for a solution.

The church in Africa works under the handicap of having some leaders who are not citizens. An American is at a special disadvantage these days and his motives are often questioned—especially by those of European origin. Too many Europeans in Africa still think of religion as something separate from the "affairs of life." They resent the "interference" of the clergy in the practical, everyday affairs of the business or political world. In spite of this resistance, the church *must* perform a reconciling mission.

There are many areas where reconciliation is needed: between Protestants and Roman Catholics, Christians and Moslems, Christians and Animists; among different branches of Protestantism; among the established churches and the sects; among the races, tribes, and age groups; even between conservatives and liberals.

I rejoice in the creative leadership of his Holiness, the late Pope John XXIII, in trying to come to a better understanding with his "separated brethren." Separation may take place in a brief period, but the knitting together takes decades—even centuries. In spite of the differences which separate, each Christian must carry in his heart continuously the reconciling love of Christ which, through forgiveness, heals wounds and knits together the divided fragments of the church universal. From the Protestant viewpoint, *rapprochement* is easier in the predominantly Protestant countries of Africa than within those under the religious orbit of Rome. It is inevitable, however, that the personal and spiritual warmth of Pope John will eventually find its way to isolated African communities. Even before that happens, Protestants everywhere must take the initiative in establishing and maintaining friendly relationships with all who adore the name of Christ.

Moslems outnumber Christians in Africa by something like three to one—a well-known fact, often forgotten. In the area under my special consideration, northern Mozambique is the only place where they are a majority. There is a sprinkling of professing Moslems almost everywhere so there is nearly always a possibility of contact. Although discussions between Moslems and Christians have been going on for years in the Near East and North Africa, there have been few in the southern part of the continent. Amicable relations are important, however, even though no major problems exist at the present time.

Animism is not a thing of the past. With the rise of pan-Africanism, there has been a resurgence of animistic beliefs and practices. An African friend (a doctor now deceased) told me that he found more reality in approaching Deity through ancestors than through Jesus Christ. Unless the church is awakened to what is happening, animism may make renewed claims for African loyalty. For the sake of understanding the past, as well as creating an opportunity for presenting the gospel, many contacts should be established with those who hold animistic beliefs. Mutual stimulation and new understanding can come out of encounters with non-Christian religions.

The relationships among the different branches of Protestantism in Africa are generally good. Some denominations which do not have much fellowship in their own countries draw close together in Africa. It is something like the meeting of two Americans in Timbuktu; they had not known each other in their home cities, but the distance between Buffalo and Boston shrinks to nothing when they meet on foreign soil. In the same way, differences which may hold denominations apart in America or Europe become minimal in Africa. Nevertheless, when a well-known branch of a world church refuses to permit a sister church to hold a meeting in its denominational edifice, there is room for improvement! Happily, national Christian councils, conferences, and alliances are bringing various groups together in mutual endeavor and fellowship.

With the growth of the so-called separatist churches in southern Africa, the problems of division become acute. Although the established churches sometimes take an attitude of superiority and aloofness, the time of drawing together may not be far off. These independent groups have a contribution to make to the older churches and vice versa. The report from Mindolo suggests that "such bridge-building takes a long time. It is often past history which has to be slowly overcome. . . . Dialogue has to be sustained on a basis of independence and mutual respect. . . . There is a great opportunity for missionaries to work in this field, provided they do it at the invitation of the independent churches and in ways which respect their cherished autonomy."

The strong drive for independence in former colonial areas of Africa has made the task of reconciliation between races most difficult because of extremists in both groups. Even in so-called Portuguese Africa, where there has been a minimum of racial discrimination, the current struggle is largely along racial lines.

There are three things which Christians of all races can do to reconcile people in a hostile environment. Churches must admit to services all people seeking to worship God. Without free entrance to churches, the Christian witness is badly marred. There must not be discrimination at the altar of the church.

Another possible avenue of reconciliation is in nonracial social and sports clubs. Although these clubs do not reach a majority of the population, they do create an environment of mutual understanding and fellowship. They provide an outlet for those who participate, and are a good example for all.

No long-range program of reconciliation can succeed unless it starts building a ground of common understanding during the formative years of childhood. A nonracial society cannot be built anywhere through segregated education. School days are the beginnings of lasting friendships. People who study together and learn to live together during school days will be less likely to become problems in a multiple society. They will have learned that there are good qualities as well as bad in people of all races. They are going to make friends with individuals because of their good qualities, not because they belong to a certain race.

In a segregated educational system, it is almost impossible to form friendships of a lasting nature, outside of one's own racial group. School loyalties are such that when education is segregated, patterns of an exclusive nature are established.

At this stage in world development free association in a multiple society needs both the assent of the intellect and the emotions. Perhaps intellectual assent can be acquired in a system of segregated schools but emotional assent will not be forthcoming unless there are some common experiences during early childhood. Such experiences can best be obtained in primary school. Integrated education is the best method of obtaining an integrated, multiple society. A fourth-year high-school pupil wrote, "Men often hate each other because they do not know each other; they do not know each other because they cannot communicate; they cannot communicate because they are separated."

One of the most tragic aspects of the political changes in Africa is the bitter clash within the African community. The fragmentation of the Congo, the continued strife between members of the United National Independence Party and the African National Congress in Northern Rhodesia, the sharp rivalry between the Popular Movement for the Liberation of Angola and the Union of Angola Peoples (both within and without Angola), all indicate the need for continuing to work for reconciliation.

The present pattern of churches overlapping tribal areas is good, although at times it may lead to friction. The church must maintain her universality while understanding the desire of individuals and groups for recognition. Insofar as possible, a balance of power must be maintained between competitive groups until tribal feelings are less pronounced and tribal differences are swallowed up in a greater loyalty.

An awareness of the divisions of the past, along with an attempt to understand and bridge these divisions, is highly important.

Age-group differences continue to be acute for the church in Africa. They can be met with understanding and a deliberate attempt to bring together various age-group representatives for discussions. As everywhere in the world, African youth feel that adults fail to listen to them or give them a chance to speak. Leisurely conferences can remedy this situation to the satisfaction and profit of both groups. The mature leaders of the church and community have an amazing amount of wisdom from the informal school of life. The youth have vitality, keen perception and often an unusual amount of information about their environment. A friend visiting Africa recently remarked with astonishment over the political acumen of African youth, "Why, even a schoolboy or a taxi driver without much formal education can discourse on political matters in a way that would astonish an American professor of political science—used to the lackadaisical interest of many American college students!" This is undoubtedly an overstatement, but African youth *are* keen observers and alert students, eager to contribute to the affairs of the church and the nation. Each age-group has its contribution to make.

The gap between so-called conservatives and liberals is a serious one. It exists more among Europeans than among Africans—quite often it is a matter of emphasis and semantics. Even the terms "conservative" and "liberal" do not carry the same meaning to all hearers. We must not allow the theological controversy, which has divided the west and followed Europeans to Africa, to deeply and permanently infect the church in Africa. Although no distinctly African theology has emerged, their world view and concept of the wholeness of life might make African independent thinkers shy away from any narrow-minded views of God and His purposes.

Wherever and whenever man meets man, there will be differences; and as long as the church exists, there will be a need for reconciliation.

21

Witness

DISUNITY IS DULLING the cutting edge of Christianity;
that edge should always be sharp and penetrating. We must
make a strong move toward unity now, so that the pattern of
division does not solidify with the stabilization of society under
new African governments—or a divided church may be bypassed
as more vital institutions are formed in the new Africa.

If the desire for unity by the majority of African Christian
leaders is not realized, the responsibility must rest largely upon
the European denominational administrators in Africa and their
supporting societies overseas. I believe (although a European
can often be completely mistaken in reading the minds of the
African people) that there is a strong desire for closer cooperation among the denominations and more intimate ties with
world organizations, and for actual organic union within denominational families. It is certain that many Africans decry
the fact that western church divisions have been foisted upon
them.

The youth, as usual, are especially outspoken. The All Africa
Christian Youth Assembly meeting in Nairobi in December,
1962, stated in a Working Party on Prayer and Worship report:

> We . . . ask that the treasures of the past be not hidden from
> us by denominational prejudice. We do not wish to worship
> as Presbyterian, Orthodox-, Reformed-, Lutheran-, Pentecosta-
> list-, Congregational-, Quaker-, Baptist-, Methodist-, or what-
> have-you-Christians, but as His people, Worshipping Him with
> the totality of our lives, using *the whole* of our inheritance to
> bring glory to His name.

The Working Party on Unity stated:

> In all humility and respect and with our pledge of loyalty
> to our churches and our leaders, we the Christian Youth meeting
> in Nairobi, Kenya, in the All Africa Christian Youth Assembly,
> call upon the churches in Africa to take positive steps which
> may create a suitable climate for conversation between Chris-
> tians and Churches to move towards unity.

The Assembly in its final message brought forth in clear and
concise terms this call of youth for unity:

> We urge the leaders of our churches to move forward with
> an extreme sense of urgency towards this goal that our Lord has
> set for us. We of the younger generation shall support them in
> this and shall, in obedience to Him, dare to take responsible
> risks where necessary.

The inaugural Assembly of the All-Africa Conference of
Churches held in Kampala, Uganda, in April, 1963, with some
350 delegates from forty-two different nations, expressed the
desire of African churchmen for Christian unity although not
necessarily for church union.

Closer ties are also desired by the supporting churches, if
one can judge by attempts which are currently going on among
them in India, Europe, and America. The movement toward
division appears to have spent its force and the pendulum
seems to be swinging in the opposite direction. In the stable
European countries there are those who feel that a divided
witness may be more effective, but the mother-churches seem
to give at least a nod of approval to proposals of closer unity
both at home and abroad.

Some European church leaders in southern Africa are mildly
interested in beginning discussions which might lead to greater
cooperation and closer unity. That interest, however, does not
have the enthusiasm or urgency expressed by the youth.

The church must turn to the New Testament in an issue as
important as this. That different groups were divinely led to
come to Africa, no one will question. That they have made a
definite contribution to the development of the continent has
been positively attested. The big question is: Is God calling

them to consolidate their efforts now that the pioneer phase is past? What does each separate group feel about Jesus' prayer "that they all may be one" (JOHN 17:21, KJV)? Each denomination will have to decide this matter for itself; for me, the call is clear—a move toward unity in two stages.

The first stage would be the organic union of different churches within the same denominational family. The British Baptists and the Canadian Baptists might well join with the Portuguese Baptists in Angola to form a single witness, following the Baptist ritual and tradition. In Mozambique at least four branches of Methodism could carry a united witness of the Wesleyan tradition. In Southern Rhodesia American and British Congregational churches, the several branches of Methodism, the various Baptist groups, the different Presbyterian churches, might come together, each in organic denominational unity. Perhaps some of the Pentecostal groups might do the same.

The Dutch Reformed Mission has only recently divided, making a European church and an African church. Perhaps it is too much to hope at this time that all of the Reformed Church groups might get together. The Anglicans have remained fairly well united wherever they have gone, as have the Seventh Day Adventists. Of course, Roman Catholics have maintained their identity with the overall loyalty to Rome although, from reports, there certainly is room for closer unity among the various orders within Roman Catholicism.

If this could be realized, there would at least be denominational unity under the canopy of world denominational organizations. It would help to remove the present denominational overlapping and confusion, such as two Methodist bishops and two Methodist chairmen of districts traveling around over the same area, each responsible for his own denominational organization.

The second stage might see the further union of churches with a fairly common theological outlook and supporting traditions. One group might consist of the liberal or semi-liberal tradition. However, the Student Christian Fellowship of the University College in Salisbury has found that:

There is more difference of belief within most denominations than between them. . . . The various beliefs of our members are not dependent on, or consistent with their denominations. Does this also apply to the churches of Southern Rhodesia? How many Methodists understand or subscribe to Wesley's view of perfection? or Presbyterians to predestination? Has not a low church fundamentalist Anglican, for example, more in common with certain sections of the Methodist and Presbyterian churches than with certain sections of his own?

The more conservative theological groups might come together to maintain their united witness in terms of their own orientation. There might be another grouping of those churches with more informality of worship and greater freedom of spontaneous expression in obedience to the leading of the Spirit.

A major group would be the Roman Catholics; it does not appear likely that serious interconfessional discussions looking toward union of Catholics and Protestants will occur within the lifetime of the present generation. As a step toward cooperation, I would like to see Rome afford Protestants the same freedom in predominantly Catholic countries, as is granted the Catholics in predominantly Protestant countries. The exclusion which the Roman Catholics practice in such countries as Spain, Portugal, Italy, and several South American countries will operate adversely against a great church in the long run, and its immediate effect is harmful to the witness of world Christendom.

The policy currently followed in some countries by the Roman Catholic Church in relation to minority Protestant groups is an open denial of the very essence of the gospel. But, until the Roman doctrine that error must give way to truth (as interpreted by the Roman Catholic Church) is superceded by Christ's teaching: "Thou shalt love thy neighbour as thyself" (MATTHEW 22:39, KJV), there can be little hope for an evangelistic thrust of a united Christendom.

I cannot visualize much hope for Christendom with the current sects and churches numbering more than a thousand, but I can see possibilities of a few great families of churches. The Society of Friends has made its major impact in Kenya; elsewhere they are making a big contribution with the work of their Service

Committee but appear to have less success in establishing a strong church.

The possible pattern of future development suggested here would give individuals plenty of choice in worship, provide a more unified witness and reduce overhead administration costs considerably.

In suggesting the above groups, I have borne in mind that Africans, like other people, differ from each other. That which appeals to one may not appeal to another. On the other hand, no one would argue that the multiplicity of forms, orders and organizations now in existence are needed to satisfy the religious nature of people in Africa.

It is to be hoped that any future churches or groups of churches in Africa will be supranational. Nothing more tragic could happen to the church than to allow itself to fall under the control of a political party. The church must always be free to bear its witness within a nation but, to be assured of this continued right, it is imperative it maintain ties outside the nation as well. In no instance should it become a tool in party politics. Its purpose is to witness to the truth as found in the Scriptures. Therefore, let us make that witness effective in unity.

A Call to Commitment

I HAVE TRIED to be faithful in presenting the anguished cries of concern, the bitter denunciations of disillusionment, the feverish proclamations of resentment which I have heard made against the church. They have hurt deeply.

I have tried to evaluate positively the contribution of the church and have been amazed at what my predecessors and colleagues have been able to accomplish at tremendous sacrifice. Could I live my life over, I would choose again to be one of them.

In anticipating the future of the church in Africa I am subdued, but not dismayed; concerned but not pessimistic; bewildered and hopeless in my own human frailty—but confident in God's grace. I have tried to suggest certain possible avenues of advance, not as though I had any private channel to the divine throne, but more as a rational outgrowth of the consideration of the church's liabilities and assets. There are many omissions and there will have to be great flexibility as dedicated people sit down and try to discover the mind of Christ in every living situation. If there is a basic commitment to God, His mind *can* be found.

The challenge to the church, therefore, is one of commitment. The church is God's instrument for the progressive and permanent salvation of His people. It is an institution which seeks to serve and, through Christ, to save. But an institution has no life apart from those who belong to it. So, the challenge is not to the church as an institution but rather to those individuals who comprise its membership—to *you* and to *me*. *Our* response will help determine its future in Africa and around the world.

A call to commitment can have only one meaning: a giving of

self—all of it—to God. A real commitment will cause some to go far from home, some to share more generously their personal resources, others to check more carefully their relationships with neighbors and colleagues, and *all* to find a higher plane of intellectual honesty and personal integrity in the daily affairs of life. The kind of commitment needed is a *total* one—renewable each morning with the rising of the sun.